Extreme Overvalued Beliefs

Extreme Overvalued Beliefs

Clinical and Forensic Psychiatric Dimensions

TAHIR RAHMAN, MD
WITH JEFFREY ABUGEL

OXFORD
UNIVERSITY PRESS

Oxford University Press is a department of the University of Oxford.
It furthers the University's objective of excellence in research, scholarship,
and education by publishing worldwide. Oxford is a registered trade mark of
Oxford University Press in the UK and in certain other countries.

Published in the United States of America by Oxford University Press
198 Madison Avenue, New York, NY 10016, United States of America.

© Oxford University Press 2024

All rights reserved. No part of this publication may be reproduced, stored in
a retrieval system, or transmitted, in any form or by any means, without the
prior permission in writing of Oxford University Press, or as expressly permitted
by law, by license or under terms agreed with the appropriate reprographics
rights organization. Inquiries concerning reproduction outside the scope of the
above should be sent to the Rights Department, Oxford University Press, at the
address above.

You must not circulate this work in any other form
and you must impose this same condition on any acquirer

Library of Congress Cataloging-in-Publication Data
Names: Rahman, Tahir, author. | Abugel, Jeffrey, author.
Title: Extreme overvalued beliefs / Tahir Rahman with Jeffrey Abugel.
Description: New York, NY : Oxford University Press, [2024] |
Includes bibliographical references and index.
Identifiers: LCCN 2024012829 | ISBN 9780197612552 (hardback) |
ISBN 9780197612576 (epub) | ISBN 9780197612583 (digital-online)
Subjects: LCSH: Extreme behavior (Psychology) | Subculture. |
Religious fanaticism.
Classification: LCC BF637.E97 R34 2024 | DDC 158—dc23/eng/20240422
LC record available at https://lccn.loc.gov/2024012829

DOI: 10.1093/9780197612583.001.0001

Printed by Sheridan Books, Inc., United States of America

Human character—this is the area where we have made the least progress—learning more about the brain, about our behavior and the ways we relate to one another.[1(p61)]

—Astronaut Neil A. Armstrong

1. Rahman T. *We Came in Peace for All Mankind: The Untold Story of the Apollo 11 Silicon Disc.* Overland Park, KS: Leathers Publishing; 2008.

CONTENTS

Preface	ix
1. Extreme Overvalued Beliefs: A Concise History	1
2. Lethal Fixations	10
3. Extreme Overvalued Beliefs	21
4. Red Flags	29
5. Anorexia Nervosa, Querulants, and Others	37
6. Lee Harvey Oswald: A New Perspective	46
7. Fame at Any Cost—Sandy Hook	63
8. Digital Subcultures	70
9. Morally Reasoned Attacks	77
10. Suicide: A Collective Identity	87
11. Extreme Overvalued Beliefs in Literature	97
Epilogue: Extreme Overvalued Beliefs and Criminal Law	105
References	111
Index	133

PREFACE

"Overvalued ideas" are designated within the pages of many well-known psychiatric textbooks as a distinct form of phenomenology. But current American psychiatric practice primarily categorizes these pathological fixations—wrongly, as we will argue in the following pages—as being due to either obsessions or delusions. Media, the lay public, and even mental health professionals will often use these terms loosely and interchangeably. This is of particular concern when discussing targeted attacks such as mass shootings or assassinations. For instance, consider individuals described as being "obsessed with guns" or as having "delusions about the government." Such individuals are usually neither obsessional nor delusional. Instead, they harbor what we call *extreme overvalued beliefs*.

The main premise of this book is that psychiatry and indeed society at large must embrace the definition of extreme overvalued beliefs to describe rigidly held, non-delusional thinking *which is shared by others*. Why? Because doing so will yield more concise definitions of violent behavior to be used in criminal proceedings, as well as aiding in the identification of perpetrators before they carry out their heinous deeds. Without a better understanding of how extreme overvalued beliefs lead to violence, the violent attacks we have come to expect on an almost daily basis will continue.

Overvalued ideas develop and evolve along a continuum, from normal fixations (such as over-the-top devotion to a certain sports team) to pathological preoccupations (such as the conviction that a local preschool is harboring a ring of child pedophiles, with no evidence to support such a notion). The ongoing challenge we face today is to understand how "normal" beliefs become dangerously overvalued, particularly subsequent to intensive online interaction, with its echo chamber free of counterbalancing views.

First, however, as a psychiatrist I must grapple with some ethical issues with regard to the cases presented in this book. These are considerations relating to the controversial 50-year-old Goldwater Rule, proclaiming that it is unethical for a psychiatrist to offer a professional opinion about an individual's mental condition unless that psychiatrist has conducted an examination of the individual and has been granted proper authorization (§7.3 of the American Psychiatric Association's [APA] Principles of Medical Ethics With Annotations Especially Applicable to

Psychiatry).[1] This rule was established as a result of *Fact* magazine's publication of remarks made by psychiatrists in the 1960s regarding Senator Barry Goldwater's mental functioning, constituting a huge embarrassment for the psychiatric profession. The debacle called into question the scientific grounding of the profession and its trustworthiness.[2,3] Similar controversies erupted in speculation about the mental fitness of President Donald Trump and concerns about President Joe Biden's cognition.[4] The rule has been written about extensively and reviewed by many noted scholars in the field.[1-5] It remains important, and I considered it carefully and discussed it with colleagues before writing this book.

It should be noted that a full history and past records on perpetrators are not always available to psychiatrists, even when they do examine them themselves. For clinical purposes, psychiatrists often, and appropriately, make do with a single in-person interview, and tele-psychiatry has become standard in the post-COVID era, in which interviews are conducted from afar. There is little theoretical or empirical support for the APA's restrictive claim that only personal examination can lead to valid diagnoses. In addition, for administrative purposes, diagnoses are made strictly from written records. Insurance companies regularly diagnose mental disorders post hoc without in-person interviews. In psychiatric malpractice cases, psychiatrists render forensic opinions without directly examining patients. This often occurs in cases of suicides, boundary violations, deaths from improperly prescribed medications, and so on. In these cases, chart reviews are accepted as the evidentiary bases for expert opinions.[1]

The cases presented in this book are meant to illustrate some alternative diagnostic conclusions. I base these conclusions on historical and factual data presented throughout this book, drawn from court documents, articles, books, and case notes provided by colleagues. This is in keeping with a more recent interpretation of the Goldwater Rule, which indicates that in some circumstances, such as academic scholarship about figures of historical importance, exploration of psychiatric diagnostic conclusions may be reasonable provided that it has a sufficient evidence base and is subject to peer review and academic scrutiny based on relevant standards of scholarship.[3] There are clearly limitations to any assessment of individuals not examined by me personally, and the conclusions here may be erroneous and are subject to my own bias. However, I believe that the cases presented here are reasonably within the ethical framework of the Goldwater Rule.

Lastly, I look at the rising death rates of young people due to eating disorders, suicides, and school shootings, which have a similar inflection point around the middle of the first decade of the 21st century to the present, coinciding with society's increasing dependence on social media. One commonalty is the notion that these behaviors are strongly influenced by shared cultural and subcultural beliefs. My aim here is to help provide a framework for pathological fixations commonly seen in psychiatry—and to provide something more nuanced that has largely been ignored, or at least underappreciated, by the field. This book, I hope, will help to sharpen the skills of forensic examiners, as well as legal and threat-assessment professionals. I hope it will also be of interest to general readers who are increasingly baffled and alarmed by the rising tide of violence and extreme behavior in our communities today. The book aims to help direct the future of psychiatric classification as it relates to targeted violence—an area in which current diagnostic categories remain insufficient.

Tahir Rahman, MD

1

Extreme Overvalued Beliefs

A Concise History

> *A child who is not embraced by the village will burn it down just to feel its warmth.*
>
> —AFRICAN PROVERB

Mass shootings have become a tragic part of modern life. Place names like Uvalde, Sandy Hook, Highland Park, and others are etched into our collective consciousness forever. When high-profile individuals such as the Kennedys, Ronald Reagan, John Lennon, or Shinzo Abe are the target, the act itself takes precedence over the location. We remember by time stamping where we were and what we were doing at the moment of the crisis.

Acts of violence against innocents or perceived enemies are often construed as a predominantly American phenomenon. More than 300 mass shootings (in which four or more victims are injured or killed) took place in the United States in the first six months of 2022.[1] Nonetheless, mass shootings inspired by twisted ideologies, political extremism, or any number of other motivating factors, are a worldwide problem. (From an epidemiological view, it is more useful to classify shootings by putative causation/motives discussed in this book rather than by number of people killed. For example, data regarding the cause of an infectious agent [bacteria versus virus, etc.] is more useful than just knowing how many people died from all infections.)

In 2011, following the detonation of a vehicle bomb in front of a government building in Oslo, Norway, that killed 8, Anders Behring Breivik, dressed in tactical gear, viciously massacred 69 more people at a Labor Party youth summer camp. Breivik's attack was on a scale never before seen in Norwegian society. His criminal trial featured a debate over his odd beliefs, including that he was a Knight Templar on a mission to "save Norway" from multiculturalism. One group of mental health experts diagnosed him as suffering from schizophrenia, while another felt he exhibited a narcissistic personality disorder.[2]

Admittedly, some of Breivik's beliefs were unique and difficult to fathom. But his actions were largely prompted by adherence to a code shared by other right-wing extremists. Since that attack, Breivik has emerged as an icon for a generation of White supremacists.[3]

Other precedents around the world have influenced homegrown terror in the United States. Eighteen-year-old Payton Gendron targeted African Americans, murdering 10 during his 2022 attack at a Tops Friendly Market in Buffalo, New York. Gendron produced a 180-page manifesto prior to the attack. He also utilized a private Discord server to house a personal diary that documented his planning for the assault (see Chapter 8). His motivations, and the manifest itself, drew largely from the writings of Brenton Harrison Tarrant, whose 2019 attack on two mosques in Christchurch, New Zealand, left 51 dead and 40 injured. Like Gendron, Tarrant's racist, right-wing beliefs were extreme, reinforced through internet communication and validation,[4] and decidedly not delusional.

RECURRING THEMES

In many instances, common threads run through case details of assailants. Schools, churches, and malls are most often attacked by the archetypical lone male gunman, alienated and dysfunctional in ways that are simply not always noticed in time to prevent an attack. (However, promising new tools utilizing *proximal warning behaviors* and *distal characteristics* have been developed and continue to be fine-tuned in an effort to improve the field's ability to predict such attacks—more on these later in the book).[5,6] Inevitably, if the shooter does not take his own life, or have it taken by law enforcement, the prosecutorial wheels are set in motion. Mental health evaluations become *de rigueur*. Delusional, psychopathic, psychotic—these terms figure prominently in the lexicon of defense. No sane person can commit a terrible act of violence that is nothing less than insane, the reasoning goes, but sadly this is simply not the case.

Some suggest that all the violence is a symptom of a societal breakdown of the traditional family unit, or of supportive social systems like churches, schools, and youth clubs. The village that raises a child no longer functions as it should, they argue. Throw in mind-altering substances, and mental health issues exacerbated by social distancing, and a plague of madness emerges, seemingly rooted in a general sociological malaise.

Other explanations point to a cry for attention, even celebrity status. In 2011, Boston Marathon bomber Dzhokhar Tsarnaev made the cover of *Rolling Stone* magazine, which to some suggested an iconic status usually reserved for the famous, not the infamous.[7] To the young, alienated mind, looking cool and being infamous can be infinitely preferable to obscurity and the indifference of others.

Eighteen-year-old Salvador Ramos attacked the Robb Elementary School in Uvalde, Texas, out of "a desire for notoriety and fame," according to the Texas

House of Representatives committee report. Ramos exhibited many warning signs in the years, months, and days leading up to the school shooting, the report noted.[8]

Could these threats have been detected sooner, and tragedy averted?

Whether a tragic event involves a "sole actor," racist, or religious fanatic, the end result is often the same—mass murder. The extremist who believes that 72 virgins await him in heaven would seem to be a far cry from a sane but fixated teen posting violent fantasies online prior to committing a violent, irrational act.[9] But what if these apparently quite different individuals instead have something in common? Something that the legal and psychiatric communities have overlooked?

The answer may well lie within the realm of a firmly established but under-considered phenomenon—extreme overvalued beliefs (EOB).[10]

The radical Jihadist is motivated by a belief in martyrdom, and the righteousness of his cause—a belief reinforced by peers as a collective identity (shared sense of belonging to a group). The outcast teen may be motivated by racism, low self-esteem, or feelings of inferiority that may afflict any young person—supported and enflamed by like-minded people online. Neither of these individuals is likely insane (legally speaking), but both are moved to action by certain beliefs that are extreme, overvalued, and shared by others of the same ilk. Both have lost the sense of balance and perspective exhibited by well-adjusted individuals, even if they share, but keep under control, some version of these same beliefs.

While the introduction of EOB as a motive pertinent to forensic psychiatric evaluations may seem to be a new or novel approach, recognition of this unique mental fixation is not.[11]

In Britain, noted reference volumes in the field, such as Sims's guidebook, *Symptoms in the Mind*,[12] the *Oxford Textbook of Psychiatry*,[13] and *Fish's Outline of Psychiatry*,[14] all classify overvalued ideas as a major type of psychopathology. These texts categorize the following conditions and classifications as disorders characterized by overvalued ideas: anorexia nervosa ("I think I am too fat"); paranoid state; querulous or litigious paranoid states ("they owe me for my damages"), morbid jealousy ("my husband is cheating on me"); hypochondriasis ("I think I have cancer"); body dysmorphic disorder ("my lips and nose need surgery"); dysmorphophobia; hoarding ("it is wasteful to throw that out"); and parasitophobia ("there are bugs in my skin").[10]

By contrast, the *Diagnostic and Statistical Manual of Mental Disorders, Fifth Edition* (DSM-5-TR)[15] and other U.S. resources perfunctorily shuffle many of these disorders into the category of "delusional disorder" (with subtypes of erotomanic, grandiose, jealous, persecutory, and somatic). Thus, major categorical disparities exist between U.S. and British practice—to the detriment of the credibility of our profession.[11] It must be noted, however, that several prominent U.S. psychiatrists, including Paul McHugh[16] (Johns Hopkins), Charles Zorumski[17] (Washington University in St. Louis), and Oliver Freudenreich[18] (Harvard) have followed the British tradition of recognizing overvalued ideas as a distinct type of psychopathology, separate from delusions and obsessions. With the exception of folie à deux (i.e., a shared delusional belief), genuine delusions are generally unshareable ("extraterrestrials are communicating with me through the radio") and are associated with a disintegration of personality, while overvalued ideas are shareable and occur in an intact personality without such disintegration.[11]

EARLY EXPLORATIONS

While EOBs have surely existed as long as civilization itself, the origins of their formal definition can be traced to the 19th century. Carl Wernicke (1848–1905), the eminent German scientist and psychiatrist well known for his neurologic research and discoveries relating to aphasia, alcoholism, and structure of the brain, was one of the earliest psychiatrists to document[19,20] the concept of overvalued ideas as a cognitive driver of targeted violence and suicide.[11]

The first description of the term *overvalued idea* appeared in Wernicke's 1892 article, "Idee Fixe [Fixations]," published in a German medical journal.[19] Surprisingly, this neglected article had not once been cited in subsequent psychiatric literature in the 130-plus years since it first appeared, until recently when our team published it. Dr. Robert Bauer stumbled across it at Washington University in St. Louis School of Medicine. Bauer is a German native and also provided key translations[11] from the vernacular copy of Wernicke's 1900 psychiatric text, *Grundriss der Psychiatrie in klinischen Vorlesungen* (Outline of Clinical Psychiatry).[20] Wernicke died after a cycling accident in 1905, but his students published the second edition of his *Gundriss* posthumously in 1906. The contemporary concept of EOB has emerged from this seminal work.[20,21]

From a psychological perspective, Wernicke theorized that overvalued ideas are those that influence behavior to a pathological degree. The shift from "normal valued-ness" to overvalued-ness occurs because of a particularly emotion-laden experience (or a series of such experiences)—the loss of a job, for instance, or a relationship breakup. Normally, counteracting ideas work to balance the influence of extreme beliefs when it comes to behavior. But a dangerous lack of association with a *variety* of thoughts, some in opposition to one another, allows certain ideas to become overvalued.[11] Tuning day after day into a single, biased news network, to the exclusion of any other sources of information, is an example of how this might happen. Black-and-white thinking, or the so-called binary bias, can set the stage for extreme overvalued beliefs.[22,23]

To illustrate his point, Wernicke used Rodian Raskolnikov, the protagonist in Dostoyevsky's 1866 novella *Crime and Punishment*, as an example of overvalued thinking. Raskolnikov narcissistically believes that he can make exceptional contributions to humanity, and thus has the right to break the law, even commit murder, in pursuit of such exceptional contributions. Thus, Raskolnikov sanctions bloodshed in the name of his *ubermensch* (superman) conscience. His innate sense of his own superiority, which sets him above the crowd, is clearly an overvalued idea.[11] Raskolnikov divides men into binary categories—ordinary and extraordinary. Ordinary people must live in submission, while extraordinary men have the right to commit any crime to advance civilization. Thus, celebrated individuals forge society by their actions and have the right to eliminate others in order to make their new discoveries known to humanity. Several times throughout the novel, Raskolnikov compares himself with Napoleon Bonaparte and has great admiration for his belief that murder is permissible in pursuit of a higher purpose, stating, "I wanted to become Napoleon." Norwegian terrorist Anders Breivik also expressed great admiration for Napoleon in his pre-attack manifesto: "He who saves the country, violates no law."[24(p171)] While Dostoevsky's character and Breivik lived in different centuries, their like-minded, grandiose views regarding moral righteousness produced violent attacks. Digital subcultures now reinforce similarly dangerous shared beliefs much more rapidly (prevalent via online forums and social media "likes" today).

There are many examples Wernicke could have drawn from to make his point. His choice of Raskolnikov was likely indicative of the novel's popularity at the time, and perhaps a desire to frame his theories within the context of familiar examples. But he also drew from a real-life case involving a passionate fixation. He cited the case of a 40-year-old unmarried female science teacher at an all-girls school who believed that a male colleague was interested in her romantically. She often spotted him gazing at her through a window in her classroom, and random encounters seemed to confirm his unwanted interest in her. It was common for her students and colleagues to think the two were in a relationship, and this reinforced her belief. She was convinced that he would propose to her, but she also admitted that there was no clear evidence that he intended to. Female colleagues expressed disdain and at other times were sympathetic, and she believed they were responsible for interfering with his true intentions. Eventually, she was admitted to a psychiatric hospital after creating a violent disturbance with the school's director and was declared insane.

Wernicke, on examining the woman, stated that she did not strike him as odd, either in behavior or her expressions, and the news that she had been declared terminally insane by the director of the institution astonished him. The woman recovered after the man left the school for an overseas trip. Wernicke concluded that there was no "psychopathic basis" for her "sexually colored" overvalued idea.[11]

Unrequited love can produce passionate, fixated beliefs and emotions—particularly in individuals with narcissistic, hysterical, paranoid, or psychopathic personality traits. While it is not uncommon for individuals to erroneously believe that someone wants to be in a relationship with them, overvalued beliefs can progress to an intense emotional commitment resulting in violence. Wernicke concluded that the content of overvalued ideas can be virtually anything. Importantly, he added the caveat that overvalued ideas are *shared* and, in many instances, normative for a society through its universal moral values such as honor, modesty, cleanliness, and beauty.[11] Such values are not themselves necessarily extreme, but clearly could be taken to extremes when enforced by an oppressive religious community or political regime. The molding of beliefs around varying cultural context is referred to as its *pathoplasticity.*

Other overvalued ideas, such as the perception of having been "slighted or judged unfairly by the government or a court"[11] may trigger *personal grievance and moral outrage*, two important drivers of violence in the context of EOBs (discussed further in Chapter 4).[6] When several individuals all perceive they have been wronged in a similar way (for instance, having been too heavily or unfairly taxed by the government), they may coordinate their actions under the aegis of their shared beliefs.[11] The result can be anything from a class action suit to a full-blown revolution.

The shift from preoccupation to pathology does not happen automatically, Wernicke added. Special conditions must prevail before such overemphasis takes on an aberrant character. Normally there is contradictory evidence which gradually corrects any overvaluation—sure, I don't like paying taxes, but apparently everyone must and does, so I suppose I'll let my grievance go. For aberrant overvaluation, however, these counterarguments, demonstrably, are no longer accessible.[19] One surrounds himself exclusively with others who refuse to pay taxes and are willing to commit violent acts in the service of the belief that taxes are unfair. The result is an *Ueberwerthige Idee*, an extreme overvalued idea.[22] Wernicke characterized overvalued ideas as appearing completely normal to the person harboring them. However, he explains, individuals may acquire an aberrant character and behavior. His examples from the late 19th century to the early 20th century included people who committed suicide after the loss of a fortune, after being sentenced to dishonorable punishment, or after the death of a loved one.[11,20]

Subsequent psychiatric literature has applied this definition to describe the psychopathology seen in other disorders with over-idealizing values including, as mentioned, anorexia nervosa, as well as body dysmorphic disorder, hypochondriasis, hoarding, morbid jealousy, litigious paranoid state, pseudocyesis (false pregnancy), and social phobia.[12,22,23]

Wernicke's description speaks to beliefs described by today's FBI profilers as the motive of many mass shooters, terrorists, and assassins that have acted in an unpredictable and violent fashion.[26] Despite the familiar image of a heavily armed teen dressed in black, psychologists, economists, and others to date have failed to establish a specific personality profile or situational condition (e.g., poverty, oppression, or lack of education) that explains terrorism. Nor does such behavior always meet classic personality disorder criteria seen in criminal psychopathology, such as antisocial personality disorder. Instead, individuals are often vaguely and unsatisfactorily described as having "psychosocial problems."

REFINING THE DEFINITION

Two important societal conditions have developed since Wernicke first described the overvalued idea: access to information (particularly online), and access to much more lethal types of weapons.[22] Applying Wernicke's concept to the development of extreme overvalued beliefs, a pathway to violence can be described as follows:

- There exists a core set of beliefs normally shared by others in one's culture/subculture.

- As the individual is exposed to progressively more extreme information and fails to consume any contradictory information, reinforcement and refinement of the extreme beliefs occur.
- Additional amplification is acquired and coupled with the use of harm to self and/or others in its service.

After Wernicke's death, the most influential philosophical work regarding overvalued ideas emerged from the German-Swiss psychiatrist and philosopher Karl Jaspers. Jaspers valued science a great deal and surmised that some mental disorders derive from brain diseases (something broken). But he also recognized that psychiatric disorders are a description of what we outwardly observe. He reminds us of the abstract nature of our diagnoses and the fact that they do not necessarily correspond fully to disease states.[22,25] As we shall see, odd or bizarre thinking either can largely be an aspect of one's unique mind (psychology/personality/culture) or can stem mainly from abnormal biological changes as a result of a mental disease.[26]

The mind and its relevant *psychological* factors are responsible for the thinking of a *violent true believer*, a term first employed by psychologist J. Reid Meloy.[26] Violent true believers are committed to an ideology that views the killing of others or oneself as a legitimate means of furthering a particular goal.[24,26] Violent true beliefs are decidedly not rooted in defective genes or damaged brains. The 9/11 terror attacks provide the most obvious and chilling example to date. We'll examine others in later chapters.

Building on Wernicke's definitions, Jaspers produced an elegant analysis of how the form and content of an overvalued idea differs from delusions. He described overvalued ideas as strongly toned by emotions, and relatable when viewed within the context of a person's personality, biographical history, and narrative. Delusions, by contrast, are not sufficiently understood as part of the person's personality or situation, but are part of a disease process which is accompanied by other cardinal symptoms like hallucinations and severe speech disorganization. Most importantly, he pointed out that overvalued ideas can occur in the presence of personality disorders *and* in healthy people.[16,27,31] This is of critical importance when discussing the motivation behind targeted violent attacks.

Wernicke's work was carried forward not just by Jaspers but also by his student, the notable German psychiatrist Kurt Schneider, and later by Professor Andrew Sims at the Royal College of Psychiatrists in London. Sims applied Jaspers's theory to examine the question, "Is Faith Delusion?" He concluded that faith is not itself a delusion as long as it is not out of keeping with one's cultural and social background (sound familiar?). However, he also underscored the notion that a highly abnormal religious belief could sometimes be regarded as an overvalued idea.[28] Once again, the September 11 attacks come to mind.[16] These coordinated attacks were carefully planned and carried out by violent true believers who did not have defective genes or brains; instead, they had developed an ideology that was refined through time and which had become increasingly binary, simplistic, and absolute.[26] They created their own extreme version of Islam and promoted many anti-Semitic and anti-Western beliefs.

In the wake of these horrific attacks, Professor Paul R. McHugh, former psychiatrist-in-chief at Johns Hopkins Hospital, invoked Wernicke's *overvalued idea* and clearly differentiated it from a delusion and an obsession[16]:

> An overvalued idea is a thought shared with others in a society or culture, but in the patient, held with an intense emotional commitment capable of provoking dominant behaviors in its service. An overvalued idea differs from a delusion in that delusions are false ideas unique to the possessor, whereas overvalued ideas develop from assumptions and beliefs shared by many others . . . the subject does not fight an overvalued idea but instead relishes, amplifies and defends it.[16(p243)]

Notions of delusion differ in various international psychiatric guides. They are usually considered demonstrably untrue or not shared by others, usually based on incorrect inference about external reality, and are typically fixed, false, and idiosyncratic. By contrast, obsessions are defined as recurrent and persistent thoughts, urges, or images that are intrusive and unwanted—causing marked anxiety or distress. The classic example is the compulsive handwashing observed in people with an obsessional fear of contagion. The individual often attempts to ignore or suppress such thoughts, urges, or images, or to neutralize them with some other thought or action (i.e., by performing a compulsion).[15] Obsessions are not nurtured and protected as are extreme overvalued beliefs.

On January 6, 2021, around 2,500 supporters of Donald Trump attacked and infiltrated the Capitol building in Washington, D.C. Eventually, around 1,000 people were charged with assaulting, resisting, or impeding law enforcement officers and/or federal employees, including more than 75 who were charged with using a deadly or dangerous weapon or causing serious bodily injury to an officer.[29] The overvalued idea that virtually all of these violent true believers shared sprang from a subculture of mainstream conservative politics—one that became increasingly simplistic, binary (*us* vs. *them*), and absolute. The idea, of course, was the lie that Donald Trump was the "true" winner of the 2020 presidential election.

Professor Hagop Akiskal of the University of California at San Diego wrote of such beliefs, "the definitive test (of a delusion vs overvalued idea) is whether an unusual belief is shared by members of the patient's subculture . . . overvalued ideas are fanatically maintained notions, such as the superiority of one sex, nation, or race over others."[30(p377)] This is best illustrated by examining the attitudes of people following the 9/11 attacks and the U.S. Capitol attack. Those who shared the hijackers' belief that the West was "at war with Islam" regarded them as heroes. Similarly, those who shared the belief that the election was stolen from Donald Trump minimized the actions of insurrectionists. Harvard psychiatrist Oliver Freudenreich explains, "While most people would not jeopardize their careers or lives for overvalued ideas, some will (and are secretly regarded as heroes by those less inclined to fight for an idea)."[31(p6)] Indeed, some Muslims overseas were seen cheering the 9/11 attacks, while some Americans minimized the U.S. Capitol attack as being perpetrated by "tourists."

In 2020, in an effort to establish a new category of fixated beliefs, an extensive body of psychiatric literature was translated from original sources and reviewed; the result was this definition of extreme overvalued beliefs (EOBs):

> An extreme overvalued belief is one that is shared by others in a person's cultural, religious, or subcultural group. The belief is often relished, amplified, and defended by the possessor of the belief and should be differentiated from an obsession or a delusion. The belief grows more dominant over time, more refined and more resistant to challenge. The individual has an intense emotional commitment to the belief and may carry out violent behavior in its service.[10(Table 3)]

Extreme beliefs can trigger extreme actions—the fact that others share those beliefs and likely support those actions fuels the likelihood of the actions actually taking place. In the coming chapters, we will explore how EOBs are pertinent in professional threat assessment.[32]

Despite the effort to clarify EOBs and to promote their adoption by practicing psychiatrists, as pointed out earlier, the DSM-5 inaptly describes overvalued ideas as beliefs held with "less than delusional intensity" and notably, "*not* shared by others" in their cultural or subcultural group.[15(p826)] The latest edition of the manual (DSM-5-TR) does reflect what has been a given for quite some time—that such beliefs are shared, a fact that can contribute considerably to their "overvaluedness." The manual correctly clarifies that overvalued ideas are indeed "normative to the individual's subgroup."[33]

It should be noted that beliefs are usually thought to be true because of observation or evidence. By contrast, a *value* is something considered to be good or important to an individual. In the chapters to follow, we'll look at what constitutes an extreme overvalued belief and what does not. We'll review case histories, psychological and sociological factors, legal ramifications, and empirical data, as well as what can be done to thwart the negative outcomes that too often materialize as a direct result of overvalued beliefs.

2

Lethal Fixations

A close look at the violence that has plagued the United States and the world in recent years reveals that a variety of psychiatric elements are at play. The term *delusion* is often invoked to characterize odd, unusual, or extreme beliefs within a classification system of psychosis that has evolved over time (featuring disorders such as schizophrenia, mood disorders with psychosis, etc.) However, as we shall see, the important concept of overvalued idea, largely ignored in forensic psychiatry, may better characterize perpetrators' beliefs in many cases involving targeted violence. One key component is pathological fixation—a preoccupation with a person or cause, accompanied by a deterioration in social and occupational functioning.[1] Such fixations have emerged as frequent warning signs (often, tragically, recognized after the fact) in targeted attacks—violence that is planned, purposeful, and predatory.[2] Although fixation is not a *predictor* of such attacks, its frequency among attackers prior to their violent acts provides support for its use as a *correlate* of such behavior, and the importance of considering fixation in efforts to prevent violence.[3]

Most people are familiar with the terms *delusion* and *obsession*—but may not realize that they have concise definitions. In order to provide clarity, this chapter will provide case examples of homicides that involved delusional or obsessional beliefs. Later chapters will discuss extreme overvalued beliefs.

In a study of warning behaviors across 377 perpetrators (between 2004 and 2019), an average of 81% were shown to have had a prior pathological fixation.[4] The association of such fixations with other characteristics in these perpetrators is also notable. In one study of violent attacks on Western European politicians, pathological fixation along with other factors was strongly correlated with attacks.[5]

Pathological fixation appears to feature a chronic and devolving state of mind—a preoccupation that damages social and occupational engagement. For example, Uvalde, Texas, shooter Salvador Ramos, seeking notoriety, killed 19 children and two teachers. According to a Texas House committee report, he had had over 100 school absences, had failing grades, and was fired from jobs at Whataburger and Wendy's.[6] Yet the internal emotional and mental dynamics that sustain fixation, known as *cognitive-affective drivers*, and their possible causes have not been elaborated upon from a clinical and theoretical perspective until now.[4,7] Recent research has implicated three primary cognitive-affective drivers for fixations: delusion, obsession, and extreme overvalued belief.[8] These three internal drivers, which evoke and sustain a pathological fixation, can often appear strikingly similar when first assessed—but they are in fact quite distinct. This can create confusion for clinical as well as forensic examiners.[7] Let's examine two of these drivers in greater detail.

LETHAL FIXATIONS FROM DELUSIONS

Delusion is a word recognized and used universally—and often too lightly. We all seem to know someone who is "deluded" about something seemingly harmless—a conspiracy in the government, for example. But as a driver of fixation and resulting acts of violence, delusions can be anything but benign. The latest (2022) version of the U.S. *Diagnostic and Statistical Manual of Mental Disorders* (DSM-5-TR) defines delusions as "fixed beliefs that are not amenable to change in light of conflicting evidence." The previous version (2013) of the *Diagnostic and Statistical Manual of Mental Disorders* (DSM-5) defined delusion as follows:

> A false belief based on incorrect inference about external reality that is firmly held despite what almost everyone else believes and despite what constitutes incontrovertible and obvious proof or evidence to the contrary. The belief is not ordinarily accepted by other members of the person's culture or subculture (i.e., is not an article of religious faith). When a false belief involves a value judgment, it is regarded as a delusion only when the judgment is so extreme as to defy credibility.[9(p819)]

The International Classification of Diseases (ICD-11) defines delusion as:

> A belief that is demonstrably untrue or not shared by others, usually based on incorrect inference about external reality. The belief is firmly held with conviction and is not, or is only briefly, susceptible to modification by experience or evidence that contradicts it. The belief is not ordinarily accepted by other members or the person's culture or subculture (i.e., it is not an article of religious faith).[10]

Although various definitions have evolved over time, forensic psychiatrists should pay close attention to the concept of delusions as "fixed, false beliefs." In some cases, delusions are often easily detected. For instance, a patient with schizophrenia may believe that nurses are trying to poison him with medications. In other cases, clinicians are left to decide the veracity of a belief. Take, for instance, a patient's belief that his wife is having an affair. This could be true, but if several family members insist it is false, the question of a psychotic mental illness must be addressed. Religious and cultural beliefs can be difficult to evaluate without intricate knowledge of the individual's subculture. The ultimate question of whether a belief is false is often a subjective one and is not easily measured scientifically. However, forensic psychologist Mark Cunningham has proposed a new model to help differentiate delusional disorder from radicalization of extreme beliefs. The model has 17 items and still needs further validation.

For this book, I have used the description traced back to Karl Jaspers, who emphasized their subjective certainty (conviction), incorrigibility (resistance to counterargument), and impossibility of content. Jaspers also argued that true delusions, as distinguished from other related phenomena, lie beyond "intersubjective understandability." In other words, delusional beliefs are meaningless to others.[11]

By Jaspers's definition, delusions can be defined as fixed, false, and *idiosyncratic* beliefs (e.g., "government spies are reading my thoughts using radio waves"). This emphasizes that they are *unique* to the individual that has them and are *not* part of a broader belief shared by others (including online). In some cases, the delusion can be "secondary," as derived from a preceding hallucination. For example, a patient with auditory hallucinations may come to believe that a device is implanted in her head as a way of "explaining" the voices she is hearing. Delusions are also frequently associated with severe mental illnesses such as schizophrenia and mood disorders accompanied by psychosis.[11-17] In forensic cases, a court often makes the final determination of an individual's beliefs. In the case of Anders Breivik, the court ruled that his beliefs matched those of right-wing extremists.[18] Clinicians often use the term "unspecified psychosis" when they need further longitudinal data.

German psychiatrist Kurt Schneider (1887–1967) provided an elegant description of what he prioritized as the "first rank" symptoms of schizophrenia (which we now know can also be present in depression or mania, in delirious patients, in substance-induced psychosis, and in malingering).[15,16] These symptoms are important for forensic psychiatrists to keep in mind, particularly when focusing on the content of beliefs in criminal cases involving psychosis[16,17]:

- Delusional perception (a sudden epiphany or revelation, e.g., "I knew God chose me as his prophet")
- Auditory hallucinations in which voices are heard spoken aloud (*gedankenlautworden*)
- A running commentary of voices, or voices arguing with each other
- Thought insertion (e.g., are thoughts put into your mind that are not your own?)
- Thought broadcasting (e.g., can you feel your thoughts broadcast or transmitted to others?)
- Thought withdrawal (e.g., do you feel your thoughts are taken away?)
- Passivity experiences (e.g., do you feel someone or something controlling your mind or body?)

Isolated delusions without other cardinal symptoms of schizophrenia or a mood disorder *do* exist as delusional *disorder*.[9(p90)] What are known as *negative symptoms* may include social withdrawal that leads to further impaired social functioning; however, in the context of targeted violence, surreptitiously planning for an attack should not be confused with social withdrawal, and should be eliminated as a sign of psychosis.[7,17]

History is replete with cases wherein delusion served as the driver of fixation and subsequent violence. But the 1843 legal case of Daniel McNaughton established the precedent of how delusional beliefs are considered by the courts for the insanity plea. Before we dive into McNaughton, though, let's first talk about *delusional disorder*.

DELUSIONAL DISORDER OR DISORDERS WITH OVERVALUED IDEAS?

Psychiatrist George Winokur (1977) described a clinical condition that he called "delusional disorder" in 29 out of 21,000 (0.4%) patients seen at the University of Iowa Hospitals between 1920 and 1975. Most of the patients he describes were individuals with beliefs concerning marriage, plots, jealousy, and persecution. He described them as having delusions without other symptoms, "nothing more and nothing less."[19] He posed the question, "Are they part of the schizophrenia spectrum?" and called for further study. Some of his descriptions of these cases bear striking resemblance to British descriptions of "disorders due to overvalued ideas," or our EOBs described here.[20] Winokur, heavily influenced by the eminent psychiatrist Emil Kraepelin, cited previous work as synonymous with his definition of delusional disorder, including a paranoid state, delusional monomania, delusional insanity, and conjugal paranoia (cheating on a lover). While his case series are considered highly influential to the field of psychiatry, he neglected to recognize that European and British scholars had previously labeled many such passionately held shared beliefs as *overvalued ideas*, which, as noted, were first described by Wernicke.[13]

Professor David Veale at King's College in London has argued that overvalued ideas are almost completely ignored by American psychiatrists, who call these overvalued beliefs delusions, often marking poor insight (inability to be objective about oneself) as the distinguishing feature.[21] Winokur's (1977) research on delusional disorder was adopted by the DSM-III committee, a diagnosis which endures in the DSM-5.[13] Over the years, though, psychiatrists have been critical of the limited scientific data surrounding delusional disorder; Harvard professor of psychiatry Theo C. Manshreck argued that "there is some question as to whether such patients are truly delusional rather than highly impressionable."[22(p1044)] If we are to gain a better understanding of the motive behind most acts of targeted violence, it is now critically important that forensic psychiatrists begin to properly identify a defendant's belief as either a fixed false conviction (a delusion) or as an intense emotional commitment to a commonly held belief shared by other members of his or her cultural group (an overvalued idea).[23]

Now let's examine some case histories involving delusions as cognitive-affective drivers of fixation.

DOWNING STREET, LONDON

On January 20, 1843, Daniel McNaughton concealed two percussion guns in his waistcoat pockets and made his way to London's Downing Street, where with one of the pistols he shot Edward Drummond, the secretary to Prime Minister Robert Peel, just below the shoulder blade. McNaughton removed and aimed his other pistol but was wrestled to the ground by constable James Silver as the second shot discharged onto the pavement. McNaughton was quickly subdued and arrested. Drummond died five days later. Multiple experts testified that McNaughton held persecutory delusions (called *monomania* in the 1800s), moving him to believe that "crews" of "spies" were following him and trying to murder him. The experts opined that he was insane, based on their examination, along with collateral information gathered from his father and other witnesses. The prosecution did not present a challenge to McNaughton's insanity defense, and the court ordered his confinement to Bethlem Hospital (known as Bedlam), where he died 22 years later.[24-26]

Some 15 experts examined McNaughton and produced evidence for trial, all arguing that the defendant was insane. After his arrest, McNaughton indicated that he thought he had shot Prime Minister Peel but was told that he actually shot Drummond. The 30-year-old McNaughton made only one public statement at London's Bow Street magistrates court:

> The Tories in my native city have compelled me to do this. They follow me and persecute me wherever I go and have entirely destroyed my peace of mind. They followed me to France, to Scotland and all over England. In fact, they follow me wherever I go. I can get no rest from them day or night. I cannot sleep at night in consequence of the course they pursue towards me. I believe they have driven me into consumption. I am sure I shall never be the man I formerly was. I used to have good health and strength, but I have not now. They have accused me of crimes of which I am not guilty; they do everything in their power to harass and persecute me; in fact they wish to murder me. It can be proved by evidence-- that's all I wish to say at present.[24(p49)]

McNaughton believed that his persecution proceeded from the priests at a Catholic church and he later complained to a commissioner that the "Tories had joined the Catholics" to persecute him. McNaughton begged his father to involve the authorities in order to have the imagined crews stop following him. McNaughton's work declined due to his symptoms, and he closed his woodturning business around the same time the delusions began. He never married and had no children. His records at Bethlem indicate "chronic mania and dementia," and that he was an avoidant person with paranoid thoughts.

Dr. J. Richard Ciccone, professor of forensic psychiatry at the University of Rochester, has retraced McNaughton's steps in London over the past several years and applied modern criteria to his case. He makes a compelling argument that McNaughton would have likely been diagnosed by modern psychiatrists with schizophrenia, because he experienced delusions and negative symptoms (social withdrawal) for longer than one year, thus meeting current DSM-5 criteria.[25] Some have said that McNaughton would have been diagnosed with delusional disorder today, but this is a rarely seen diagnosis (more on this in Chapter 3). McNaughton's beliefs were proven through witness testimony to be fixed, false, and idiosyncratic; no other Englishman in 1843 believed that Catholic and Tory "crews and spies" were following him "day and night" as McNaughton did. He was alone in his beliefs, and as such we can say they were delusions.[24,25]

The McNaughton trial provoked an outcry in the newspapers, and from no one less than Queen Victoria herself. Questions were put to the 12 judges of the Court of Common Pleas by the House of Lords, the answers to which would come to be known as the McNaughton (also called M'Naughten) Rules. This 1843 insanity test is well known to all students of British common law: "To establish a defence on the ground of insanity it must be clearly proved, that, at the time of committing the act, the party accused was labouring under such a defect of reason from disease of the mind, as not to know the nature and quality of the act he was doing, or if he did know it, that he did not know that what he was doing was wrong."[26(p226)] The McNaughton case is important mainly because it involved isolated symptoms of delusions, and it continues to this day to influence legal thinking regarding the insanity defense.[24-26]

In a contemporary case, 66-year-old Dante Soiu of Ohio developed an erotomanic delusion that drove his fixation on the actress Gwyneth Paltrow: the chronic psychotic belief that she was in love with him.[5,27] He had seen her in a movie, and that same day he also saw her photo on the cover of a magazine at the grocery store. He felt certain that this was no coincidence but rather a "sign" meant especially for him—a psychotic symptom called a *delusion of reference*.[16] At night, he claimed, he would answer his telephone and be confronted with silence. He *knew* that it was her on the other end—he believed she could not talk because of her mother's disapproval of their relationship, but with her silence was letting him know that she loved him. Fueled by these psychotic symptoms, over the next several months he sent her numerous sexualized letters, sex toys, gifts, and packages, and then traveled on two occasions to visit her at her parents' home in Santa Monica—despite an FBI agent ordering him to cease his behavior between the first and second trips. On the second visit, he was arrested and charged with stalking.[4]

The man was forensically evaluated by J. Reid Meloy on two occasions: during his trial and after eight years of confinement in various California forensic hospitals. Schizophrenia was ruled out as a diagnosis given the absence of formal thought disorder, hallucinations, and any other negative symptoms; he was instead diagnosed with delusional disorder, erotomanic subtype (a form of delusional disorder in which an individual believes that another person, usually of higher status, is in love with him). In the highly publicized trial, he was found not guilty by reason of insanity (NGRI), and subsequently was determined not to pose a risk of violence toward Ms. Paltrow. But after several years of release into the community under the care of his brother, he resumed his attempts to contact her and consummate their relationship. His erotomanic delusion persisted. Although he had received various psychotropic medications, such as olanzapine, and psychotherapeutic interventions through his years in the hospital—and would intentionally disavow his continued fixation upon Paltrow in psychiatric interviews—his active suppression to act on his delusion following his release could not be sustained. He contacted her, although he never traveled to see her again and as such was assessed to no longer pose a physical risk of harm.[4,27]

Andrea Yates was a devoutly religious and loving mother of five children in Texas. She was valedictorian of her high school class of 600 students and later became a respected nurse. She was generally a responsible person and did not use drugs.[28]

Yates, in a highly publicized trial, was shown to suffer from a severe major depressive disorder with psychotic symptoms, requiring four hospitalizations and treatment. In 2001 she sequentially drowned her five children (aged 6 months to 7 years) by holding them face down in the bathtub at home. After her arrest, forensic psychiatric examinations by psychiatrist Phillip Resnick revealed that she experienced delusions of being possessed by a demon (cacodemonomania).[28] She believed that Satan was actually within her and that if she did not take her children's lives before the age of accountability, they would be condemned to hell, where their souls would remain for eternity. While many people believe in Satan, Yates alone believed that her children should be drowned to somehow protect their souls—making her beliefs fixed, false, and idiosyncratic. She also uniquely believed that after their murders, she would be executed for killing her children, and Satan would die from within her and bring about Armageddon. She expected to die as a righteous individual and believed that her children would be better off in heaven than on Earth.[28,29]

OBSESSIONS: INTRUSIVE AND UNWANTED THOUGHTS

In addition to delusion, a second cognitive-affective driver of fixation is obsession. It is important to first clarify the definition of obsession because laypeople and even mental health workers often use it improperly (e.g., "he was obsessed with buying guns and White supremacy"). As noted earlier, obsessions are "recurrent and persistent thoughts, urges, or images that are experienced, at some time during the disturbance, as intrusive and unwanted, and in most individuals cause marked anxiety or distress."[9(p826)] An example is the young man stricken with an extreme fear of germs who washes his hands until they bleed; or the young mother who is inexplicably bombarded with unwanted thoughts of murdering her beloved newborn. These individuals often attempt to ignore or suppress such thoughts, urges, or images, or to neutralize them with some other thought or action (i.e., by performing a compulsion—say, ritualistic and repeated handwashing or checking for someone hiding under the bed). Obsessions are ego-dystonic (unwanted and distressing)—the young mother would never harm her baby—rather than ego-syntonic (compatible with the self, and often an element of one's identity).[4] A White supremacist who relishes Nazi propaganda is not considered to be "obsessed" with it because he enjoys, amplifies, and defends it—the complete opposite of an obsession.

True obsessions are often diagnosed as obsessive-compulsive disorder (OCD) and are measurable and indeed highly treatable.[30–36] OCD often causes severe mental anguish and morbidity and is often under recognized. Many people with OCD have distressing violent images and thoughts that cause them to seek medical attention after significant delay. When they present for treatment, they are frequently misdiagnosed and even improperly committed to psychiatric hospitals. Despite the violent and aggressive thoughts associated with OCD, there is no significant evidence that these individuals are at risk of acting on their obsessions. In fact, some evidence suggests that the presence of OCD is actually *protective* against aggression.[34] OCD is treatable, and in severe cases neurosurgical electrode implantation with deep brain stimulation can be effective.[35]

People with OCD can sometimes also progress to frank psychosis.[32] Advances in neuroimaging have identified brain structures potentially involved in the neurobiology of OCD, including neurocircuits modulating emotional, cognitive, and motor control.[36] It is important to differentiate people with OCD from those who have delusions or extreme overvalued beliefs, where the presence of beliefs heralds a much greater risk that should not be ignored.[4]

Note that the popular use of the word *obsession*, such as "she is obsessed with World Cup soccer," differs from the psychiatric understanding of the term because ego-syntonic activity that is enjoyable (World Cup soccer) is not diagnosable as a true obsession. In fact, many fixations are normal and needed for human survival and success. Examples include remodeling a house, dieting, completing an education, collecting antiques, romantic relationships, and mother-infant bonding. While many laypeople may see these fixations as obsessions, they may be completely normal. However, any of these fixations can *become* clinically relevant as overvalued ideas if they cause problems in social or occupational function (dieting to the point of developing anorexia, collecting antiques instead of paying the rent). As we shall later see, fixations involving moral codes (e.g., "abortion is always murder") often have the propensity to become extreme overvalued beliefs.

Several clinical scales and interventions have been developed for OCD, including psychotherapy and several available pharmacological treatments.[30,31] But there are still questions about the demarcation between obsessions as a symptom of OCD versus of schizophrenia-spectrum psychopathology, particularly given the relationship between a diagnosis of OCD and subsequent risk for schizophrenia.[32,33]

In a forensic or threat-assessment context, fixations driven by obsessional thoughts are very infrequent and generally do not pose a risk of violence.[34] However, there is a limited body of research reaching back to the early 20th century on certain violent behaviors called *catathymic homicides*.[37-43] The term itself means "in accordance with emotions."[39(p39)] The acute form is manifest in a sudden murder without any apparent motive, and has obsessional thinking as the explanation: the individual attacks a stranger with sudden, explosive violence, and in the aftermath is consumed with guilt and no understanding of why he did it.[39-43] The obsessional fixation has an incubation stage, during which the individual is obsessed with the unwanted thought of murdering someone, and despite all conscious efforts, cannot rid his mind of the preoccupation. The second stage is a sudden homicidal act, usually in the absence of any history of violence; in the third stage, the individual experiences profound relief following the killing and his memory is fully preserved.[39-41] The pathway follows this course:

> Distressing, unwanted thought of killing → sudden, homicidal act → profound relief

The following two case histories illustrate lethal fixations from obsessions.

Case 1

A 37-year-old man, married with three sons, had been clinically depressed since adolescence. His mother had been depressed since he was 6 years old, and eventually divorced her husband and abandoned the family. Both of his maternal grandparents committed suicide. The subject was also diagnosed with a dependent personality disorder and OCD. He was disabled from his work as a bricklayer and confined to his home. He was taking a prescribed cocktail of medications for depression and OCD, including olanzapine, bupropion, venlafaxine, and lorazepam, and seeing his psychiatrist once a month. He was not currently in psychotherapy, so there was no one to ask whether he was experiencing unwanted urges to harm others.

The man's first homicidal thoughts had begun eight years earlier and were captured in a psychiatrist's note during one of four psychiatric hospitalizations: "worries whether he will kill anybody or not." The specificity of his plan did not crystallize until the morning of the murder, when it focused on his youngest, a 13-month-old son. He drowned him in the bathtub, left a note for his wife, and called the police. His explanation was that by killing one of his children, he would be free of all the pressures in his life, and his state of mind, which included feelings of desperation, humiliation for failing as a father and breadwinner, guilt, and social and occupational paralysis, would be much improved. After the homicide he reported:

> I was relieved at the time. It felt like a burden was lifted off of me. It was there for a couple of hours. Then at the jail I asked God to forgive me for killing. I realized what I did. Not a lot of emotion. A little guilt. I felt God has forgiven me. I know by faith and his Word he will forgive us our sins and cleanse us from all unrighteousness. I slept that evening.[43(p1)]

The note he left for his wife said, "I'm sorry I killed John. I couldn't do anything else. I'm not a man. I am a coward. John is lying on the bed. Here is the key to the mower. Don't let the boys have it."[43(p2)]

The subject had no history of violence or criminality. A court-appointed psychiatrist who evaluated him six weeks after the murder wrote in his report, "I have done forensic evaluations for nearly 30 years.... I have never seen a case quite like this.... His reasoning does not explain an act that was totally out of character for him."[43(p3)] Dr. Reid Meloy evaluated the subject and testified at his murder trial; the subject addressed the court prior to his sentencing to life imprisonment. He turned to everyone assembled in the courtroom of his rural Midwestern town and tearfully apologized for what he had done. In this rare case, the homicide was motivated by thoughts and actions which were unwanted, intrusive, and caused the subject marked anxiety and distress.[43]

Case 2

Charles Whitman was a 25-year-old engineering student and former Eagle Scout and Marine sharp-shooter who in 1966 inexplicably killed 17 people and wounded 30 others. Prior to the shooting from the University of Texas clock tower, Whitman first stabbed and killed his mother, then his wife. Whitman had seen a school psychiatrist, and wrote about it in a suicide letter he left on his typewriter: "I talked with a Doctor once for about two hours and tried to convey to him my fears that I felt [overcome by] overwhelming violent impulses. After one session I never saw the Doctor again, and since then I have been fighting my mental turmoil alone, and seemingly to no avail."[44(p2)]

Whitman went on to explain:

> I do not quite understand what it is that compels me to type this letter. Perhaps it is to leave some vague reason for the actions I have recently performed. I do not really understand myself these days. I am supposed to be an average reasonable and intelligent young man. However, lately (I cannot recall when it started) I have been a victim of many unusual and irrational thoughts. These thoughts *constantly recur*, and it requires a tremendous mental effort to concentrate on useful and progressive tasks.[45(p169, emphasis added)]

Whitman's description of his thoughts as recurrent and seemingly unwanted points to an obsession as part of his mental disorder, along with depressive symptoms and stimulant abuse—although the subject of his obsessive thinking is not clear. Whitman, perhaps perceiving that his mind was not working right, requested that an autopsy be performed, and his brain examined. A nickel-sized glioblastoma (brain tumor) was found near the amygdala in his brain. Experts have speculated that Whitman's emotional and behavioral control may have been influenced by this tumor.[44] There have been rare reports of obsessive-compulsive symptoms as a side effect of psycho-stimulant medications for attention deficit-hyperactivity disorders.[46]

These cases have been reviewed to emphasize the fixed, false, and idiosyncratic nature of true delusions (which forms the basis of the forensic framework I am proposing in this book—and which aligns with classic definitions).[11-14] Delusions usually occur alongside other signs and symptoms of psychotic illnesses. Obsessions, by contrast, are recurrent, and unwanted. Both are distinct from extreme overvalued beliefs as drivers of pathological fixations.

3
Extreme Overvalued Beliefs

> *In all times, and all countries especially in those countries which are divided within by religious faith, there are always fanatics who will be well contented to be regarded as martyrs.*[1]
>
> — ALEXANDRE DUMAS

Just as a delusion, or rarely an obsession, can lead to violence, so can an *extreme overvalued belief*. Such a belief is often simplistic and binary, but it is often more difficult to disprove than a delusion. The content of a belief itself and its emotional intensity can rapidly transform it from normal to extreme and overvalued. For example, one of the recruitment themes that undergird the ideology of the Islamic State is "the West is at war with Islam"—simple, binary, and somewhat difficult to disprove.[2] The terrorist organization Hamas recently carried out an attack against Israeli civilians. One of the organization's stated beliefs is that there is no negotiated settlement possible and that violent Jihad is the only answer to the Israeli-Palestinian conflict. Similarly, a potential mass shooter may harbor a moral grievance through which he identifies with other mass shooters. An extreme, passionate belief in this grievance may well lead to violent action.[3,4]

Emotions play an important role in extreme overvalued belief (EOB), and often paradoxically include both positive and negative emotional states. Lone actors and some group-based terrorists may feel moral outrage on behalf of a perceived victimized group, and vicariously identify with that group, resulting in anger, humiliation, or other dysphoric states.[5,6] For example, neo-Nazi Dylann Roof believed that Black people were taking over the world, and in response he wanted to start a civil war. He then progressed further along the pathway toward violence, his empathy growing for the "victimized" group (White people). This then kindled in him an image of the self as a warrior or soldier, dedicated to defending these supposed victims. Feelings of exhilaration, excitement, or other euphoric states may accompany this self-image.[7] Such paradoxical emotional states, attitudes, and assumptions energize the EOB and are nurtured by the extremist group, often bolstered by exposure to social media.[8] These beliefs can, in turn, drive an impulse to sacrifice the self and/or others that is bereft of any critical analysis or judgment.[8-11] These features are seen in Roof's rhetoric:

> I have no choice. I am not in the position to, alone, go into the ghetto and fight. I chose Charleston because it is most historic city in my state, and at one time had the highest ratio of blacks to Whites in the country. We have no skinheads, no real KKK, no one doing anything but talking on the internet. Well someone has to have the bravery to take it to the real world, and I guess that has to be me.[12(np)]

The neurobiological basis of such a thought process, which we refer to as a *cognitive-affective driver*, may be similar to that found in stalking.[13,14]

On the surface, eating disorders (see Chapter 5) would seem to be quite distinct from lone-actor terrorism, and indeed they are in that eating disorders virtually never provoke violence in those who suffer from them. As with the violent extremist, though, individuals with overvalued beliefs in the supremacy of the thin-body ideal do not generally walk into a clinic or emergency room wanting help; they are invested in and protect their extreme beliefs. Family and others who are close to someone with an eating disorder may be concerned, but may also dismiss the ideology as "normal" because it is shared by others in their subculture—countless women pursue the "perfect" body, to their own detriment, after all.[15] Likewise, individuals with anti-Semitic, anti-Islamic, anti-government, or anti-abortionist views may appear to be no different from those with whom they surround themselves. In fact, such individuals, like those with anorexia, do not have cardinal psychotic symptoms, making them difficult to detect and assess. Often the first signs of their "psychopathology" are late-stage markers on the pathway to violence, or a mass attack which appears spontaneous but in truth is not.[7]

Carl Wernicke argued that it was possible for any belief to become overvalued, and that an affect-laden (very emotional) experience often triggers or reinforces the belief. For instance, a depressed or grieving individual, feeling slighted by the government or by society, might convert to a new religion or begin exploring new ideologies. Such behavior might help decrease anxiety and soothe uncomfortable feelings as the new ideology becomes a source of inspiration.[16] Anders Breivik, in a dark and tragic attempt to honor the 12th-century Knights Templar order, wore US Marine military regalia and designed his own sleeve insignia, thus becoming a "warrior" in his own mind.[17,18] Such warning signs relating to identification with a militaristic or violent group are often found in targeted attackers and in the majority of lone-actor terrorists.[5,7,19] As extreme overvalued belief is an important cognitive-affective driver in many cases of mass violence, it demands a careful examination (often by piecing together information from multiple sources) of the content and intensity of beliefs, including any early or central grievance justifying violence. At the same time, a fixation driven by a delusion or an obsession must be ruled out.[20]

The following case histories illustrate extreme overvalued belief as a cognitive-affective driver.

OKLAHOMA CITY BOMBING

In April 1995, Timothy McVeigh detonated a 500-pound ammonium nitrate and fertilizer bomb in front of the Alfred P. Murrah Federal Building in Oklahoma City, killing 168 men, women, and children. McVeigh was subsequently arrested, charged, tried, and convicted. He was executed by lethal injection two months before 9/11, closing the book on the worst act of domestic terrorism in U.S. history.

Psychologist J. Reid Meloy was retained by the U.S. attorney general to assess McVeigh and his co-conspirator, Terry Nichols,[21-24] but because neither defendant entered a mental disability defense, Meloy was unable to clinically evaluate them. Voluminous evidence presented at trial indicated that McVeigh held a personal grievance toward the U.S. government over his failure to qualify for the Army Special Forces selection process conducted at Fort Bragg, North Carolina. He subsequently immersed himself in the Patriot Movement, an extreme right-wing subcultural militia. Ideologically, this group promoted a blend of anti-government, anti-abortion, anti-Semitic, pro–Second Amendment, and racist beliefs. When the Branch Davidian compound in Waco, Texas, was raided in April 1993, McVeigh was particularly outraged. He believed that federal agents deliberately murdered men, women, and children with the fires that engulfed the compound. The Branch Davidian group had been stockpiling illegal weapons, for which federal agents obtained a search warrant and arrest warrants for its leader, David Koresh. McVeigh drove to Waco during the siege to show his support. At the scene, he distributed pro–gun rights literature and bumper stickers bearing slogans such as, "When guns are outlawed, I will become an outlaw."[23-27]

The blaming of the U.S. government for the conflagration at Waco, as well as other events of that time, was the basis of key shared subcultural beliefs among the members of the Patriot Movement. Their anger was deeply felt and was magnified by earlier popular books such as *The Turner Diaries*, a novel by neo-Nazi William Pierce that provided a template for McVeigh's bombing of the Murrah Building.[24,26]

Why did McVeigh, among the many who harbored such anger and grievance, choose to commit an act of terrorism? Uniquely, McVeigh held two central and unique EOBs that drove his fixation: he would become the "ultimate warrior"; and his bombing would begin a violent overthrow of the U.S. government, culminating in his rebirth as the "first hero of the second American Revolution." These beliefs were shared with several individuals, including McVeigh's younger sister. They were relished, amplified, and defended for at least two years prior to the bombing. They became more dominant and resistant to change leading up to the attack,[22-24] and they were fueled by McVeigh's narcissistic personality.[23-25]

In the end, a grieving nation was particularly moved by the story of 19 small children killed in the blast. McVeigh later described his unsympathetic actions: "Think about the people as if they were storm troopers in Star Wars. They may be individually innocent, but they are guilty because they work for the Evil Empire."[26(np)] Clearly, McVeigh's beliefs overruled any sense of empathy.

In subsequent interviews, McVeigh's attorneys stated that they had expected to see a crazy person when they arrived to intervene. Attorney Chris Tritico said that he was "pleasantly surprised that [McVeigh] was absolutely not crazy."[27(p2)] The insanity defense was not asserted because experts found McVeigh to be competent to stand trial, and ascertained that his actions were deliberate, planned, and motivated by extremist ideology. His attorney summed it up, "He's as sane as any lawyer or reporter."[27(p1)] In fact, McVeigh, like the Unabomber Ted Kaczynski, did not want to be considered insane because of his strong convictions. Had his case gone to trial with an insanity plea, his beliefs could have been explained away by the defense as the tragic delusions of a madman. The prosecution would have had to disprove this.

Media coverage of the bombing often employed the term *delusional* or *obsessional* to describe McVeigh's motives. A more concise definition would have clarified matters, helping Americans to understand that this was not the work a lone psychotic individual. Author Jeffrey Toobin explains, in his book *Homegrown: Timothy McVeigh and the Rise of Right-Wing Extremism*, that the ideology and tactics used by McVeigh have flourished in the decades since his death in 2001, culminating in the January 6, 2021, U.S. Capitol attack.[24]

At McVeigh's trial, mental health experts could have used the term *extreme overvalued beliefs* to describe the motivation for his crime by stating the following: McVeigh held extreme overvalued beliefs at the moment he detonated the bomb in front of the Murrah Building. His actions were not delusions or obsessions.[25] Instead, his ideology was (and continues to be) shared by others in American right-wing subculture. This dangerous subculture (still present today) relishes, amplifies, and defends the idea that an army of people should rise up and defend what the Declaration of Independence proclaims, "Whenever any Form of Government becomes destructive of these ends, it is the Right of the People to alter or to abolish it." McVeigh, like many others, held an intense emotional commitment to those beliefs and carried out violent behavior toward the law enforcement agents that he targeted during his attack. He did not have a history of a severe mental disorder such as schizophrenia.[23]

A psychologist might suggest that insecure attachment (the lack of a secure bond with a close and loving caregiver) in childhood likely contributed to an adulthood more susceptible to the adoption of an overvalued extremist ideology. McVeigh sought and became overdependent on the approval and acceptance of others, first by trying to join the Special Forces and later by adopting a radical ideology. Though he couldn't pass the physically rigorous Special Forces test, McVeigh still dreamed of becoming the "ultimate warrior" he had envisioned in childhood. This resulted in an overvalued attachment to extremist ideology and ultimately McVeigh's awakening as a violent true believer. Overvalued beliefs compel targeted violence, sanctioned by an external moral code (e.g., Second Amendment rights and the belief that a tyrannical government should be held accountable for taking gun rights away).[23–28]

Notably, a failure of intimate pair bonding is a key characteristic of many lone-actor terrorists. Devoid as he was of normal loving relationships with women, McVeigh sought security instead by clinging to and relishing an overvalued belief system. His abnormal, overvalued personality organization stimulated anger, feelings of rejection, anxiety, and moral outrage, culminating in the Oklahoma attack.[22-25]

FORT HOOD ATTACK

In November 2009, former U.S. Army major and psychiatrist Malik Hasan committed mass murder at Fort Hood, Texas, killing 13 soldiers and injuring 32 others. At the time, his unit was being medically processed for deployment to Afghanistan. Hasan had become radicalized over the previous few years, evidencing his fixation through presentations during his residency program and public health fellowship, which increasingly focused on convincing others that the West was at war with Islam, with little reference to psychiatry.[29-31]

According to one formal legislative report after the massacre, one of Hasan's draft presentations consisted almost entirely of Koranic verses and references, without a single medical or psychiatric term. Hasan's draft also presented extremist interpretations of the Koran, such as supporting grave physical harm and killing of non-Muslims. He even suggested that revenge might be a defense for the terrorist attacks of September 11. Hasan's superiors warned him that he needed to revise the presentations if he wanted to graduate and concluded that they were "not scientific," "not scholarly," and mere "recitation of the Koran" that "might be perceived as proselytizing."[30,31(np)]

Was his fixation driven by delusion, obsession, or extreme overvalued belief? Following the massacre, Hasan was examined by several military forensic psychiatrists who determined that he did not have a mental disorder[29-31] and therefore did not qualify for an insanity defense. Some of his comments during his psychiatric examination implied his EOB: "I was focused . . . I had a mission to accomplish . . . I got the job done . . . I wanted to take out as many soldiers as I could before I got stopped . . . I don't think what I did was wrong because it was for the greater cause of helping my Muslim brothers . . . I regret being paralyzed . . . [the soldiers he killed] were going against the Islamic Empire."[30(np)] Hasan believed that the United States was waging an unjust war against Islam, and that "fighting for God was a noble deed."[31(p26)]

Hasan attempted to enter a "defense of others" defense at trial on the basis that the victims were part of the U.S. military; Hasan's "others" were the leaders of the Taliban with whom he identified, even though he had never met such a leader, nor had he visited Afghanistan. He defined his killings as a form of self-defense.[25] "Defense of others" requires that one was compelled to use force against an aggressor to protect a person or group from being harmed or killed by that aggressor. The persons being protected must be victims of unlawful force and face an immediate threat or danger. The judge rejected this defense as a matter of law a week after it was entered. Hasan did not present any subsequent defense, preferring to receive the death penalty and become a martyr. Central to his radicalization and motivation for his attack was his theology, which contained EOBs that obligated him to attack.[25,30]

Two features of Hasan's ideology critical to understanding his worldview were his conceptions of hell and obedience to God.[31] An all-encompassing fear of hell played an enormous role in determining how Hasan thought and acted, and he repeatedly wrote and stated that he believed hell to be a real, physical place, and that his primary motivation in committing violence was to avoid it. Hasan felt that a pious Muslim must obey God's commands without question, and that failure to do so would cause him to lose his "rank" in heaven. As he came to believe that God was commanding him to fight in His name against the enemies of Islam, Hasan, according to this worldview, was left with no choice but to comply or risk condemnation to hell. In both his own writings and as quoted in a mental evaluation conducted by a military panel over three days in December 2010, Hasan claimed that he did not want to kill soldiers, but felt compelled to do so because God commanded it. Without understanding Hasan's interpretations of hell and obedience to God, it is impossible to understand why he committed the attack.[31(pp21-22)] Hasan studied the teachings of a radical imam, Anwar al-Awlaki, who condemned any Muslim fighting against his brothers in Afghanistan and Iraq. Once Hasan's shared, radicalized religious beliefs are understood, it becomes clear that he held EOBs, and not delusions.[25] He was sentenced to die for the attack and remains detained at Fort Leavenworth, Kansas.

CESAR SAYOC

In 2018, 57-year-old Cesar Sayoc mailed 16 manila envelopes containing pipe bombs built using PVC piping, explosive material, and a small clock. The recipients included Joseph Biden, former CIA director John Brennan, former director of National Intelligence James Clapper, former secretary of state Hillary Clinton, former attorney general Eric Holder, President Barack Obama, George Soros, and others. Some of the names were misspelled (e.g., "Hilary" instead of "Hillary").[32-34]

The improvised devices that Sayoc created contained actual explosives, but were poorly made and lacked a trigger mechanism, so they didn't explode. The FBI matched a fingerprint on the bomb intended for Maxine Waters to Sayoc, who later pleaded guilty to 65 felony charges, including using weapons of mass destruction in an attempted domestic terror attack. He was placed on suicide watch in jail and received medication for anxiety. He was sentenced to 20 years in federal prison.[33]

At the time of his arrest, Sayoc was discovered to be living in a white van plastered with pro-Trump stickers and signs. One had crosshairs over an image of

Hillary Clinton, another one over the image of liberal filmmaker Michael Moore. His attorneys argued that he had limited intellectual ability, which made him susceptible to dubious stories of Democratic malfeasance. Sayoc believed that because of his stickers supporting President Trump, liberals had broken the window of his van, slashed his tires, and tried to kill him by cutting fuel lines. Mr. Sayoc reported this damage to the police. He also believed news reports that Trump supporters were being beaten in the streets and that he was being personally targeted by those he perceived as Trump's enemies. Sayoc admired Adolf Hitler and believed that Hispanics and African Americans were taking over the world. He believed that President Obama was not born in the United States. When he found out that his pizza-shop employer was a lesbian, he told her that she should burn in hell.[33,34]

Mental health experts noted that Sayoc had a severe personality disorder and that he was a victim of childhood sexual abuse, and had learning disabilities and cognitive limitations.[32–34] His father abandoned the family when he was five years old. A priest raped him when he was eleven. One expert opined that the anabolic steroids Sayoc abused to bulk up (he could bench press nearly 500 pounds) caused "roid rage." He consumed 170 vitamins a day and performed onstage in strip clubs.

At the time of sentencing, Sayoc's attorneys used the terms *obsession* and *delusion* to describe his fixations.[32,33] Alternatively, mental health experts could have described his fixations as EOBs. He relished, amplified, and defended them; what's more, Sayoc's beliefs were (and are to this day) shared by others, including many Trump supporters who later took part in the U.S. Capitol attack on January 6, 2021. In Sayoc, these beliefs, which proliferated online and through other digital means, grew more refined, more dominant, and more resistant to challenge as time went on.

But, as with McVeigh, why Sayoc? If so many people harbor such beliefs, why do so few succumb to violence as he did? It could be argued that Sayoc's loss of a primary parental figure (his father) and victimization by others resulted in an adult mental life with an unstable self-image.[35] Love is an important childhood need, and Sayoc developed overvalued attachments to compensate for its apparent absence, seeking approval and acceptance from the likes of Donald Trump rather than from a caring parent. (Sayoc's mother, meanwhile, admonished President Trump for his rhetoric of war with the media and Democrats.) Sayoc's extreme bodybuilding and his attempts to gain approval from women by performing at strip clubs would seem to reinforce this kind of overcompensation. He adopted an overvalued pro-Trump and anti–Democratic Party moral code and wished to please figures he saw on television. He became dependent on political ideology and rhetoric—which he and other supporters interpreted quite literally. When presented with alternative beliefs or subcultures (different races and views, sexual and gender minorities, etc.) Sayoc's overvalued personality organization stimulated personal outrage, culminating in his distribution of the package bombs. While his decisions seem outlandish and "bordering on delusions," they are also in keeping with his subculture's ideology—that the people he targeted should be eliminated to create a better world. While most people would not jeopardize their careers or lives for overvalued ideas, as Harvard psychiatrist Oliver Freudenreich[36] has pointed out, others with similar beliefs may secretly regard individuals like Sayoc, McVeigh, and the U.S. Capitol or Hamas attackers as heroes.

4
Red Flags

By failing to prepare, you are preparing to fail.
—BENJAMIN FRANKLIN

Pathological fixation, a preoccupation with a person or a cause that is accompanied by deterioration in social and occupational functioning, precedes most cases of targeted violence.[1] The terror attacks of 9/11 changed the world forever, and propelled governments into an unprecedented examination of violent true believers—many of whom wish to act alone in their attacks. After 9/11, a critical need to thwart future attacks arose almost overnight. The difference between idiosyncratic, psychotic thinking and shared subcultural ideologies quickly became apparent to experts in the fields of psychiatry, psychology, and threat assessment. Researchers began envisioning instruments analogous to weather warnings that would detect the conditions ripe for a "perfect storm" of violence in order to prevent future terror attacks. This would first require careful collection and analysis of data.

These efforts eventually culminated in a breakthrough—the *Terrorism Radicalization Assessment Protocol* (TRAP-18), developed by psychologist and FBI consultant Dr. J. Reid Meloy.[1-4] The TRAP-18 is a structured and validated (scientifically tested) approach for threat assessment which has undoubtedly been responsible for saving numerous lives. Today it is considered a key assessment instrument for counterterrorism professionals around the world. The case histories provided throughout this book are illustrative of the many behaviors identified in this protocol; once they are recognized, they become easy to spot when discussing attacks. More importantly, the TRAP-18 helps professionals identify potential attackers before the violence starts; it is a professional model designed for prevention, not prediction, of an attack. It has two parts: *distal characteristics* (of which there are 10) and *proximal warning signs* (of which there are 8), as shown in Table 4.1.

Table 4.1 VARIABLES FROM THE TERRORIST RADICALIZATON ASSESSMENT PROTOCOL TRAP-18 (COURTESY OF J. REID MELOY, PHD, ABPP).

Proximal Warning Signs	Distal Characteristics
Pathway	Personal grievance and moral outrage
Fixation	Framed by an ideology
Identification	Failure to affiliate with a group
Novel aggression	Dependence on the virtual community
Energy burst	Thwarting of occupational goals
Leakage	Changes in thinking and emotion
Last resort	Failure of sexually intimate pair bonding
Directly communicated threat	Mental disorder
	Creativity and innovation
	Criminal violence

The presence of a cluster of TRAP-18 distal characteristics, along with the *absence* of all proximal warning behaviors, indicates that a person *may* be at risk of committing a violent act—storm clouds on the horizon. While it may still be uncertain whether violence is imminent, in the world of threat assessment this means that the case should be monitored and reviewed on a regular basis—a severe storm watch. The case does not yet warrant more commitment of active management resources. But add *any one or more* of the proximal warning behaviors, and the violence is considered imminent—a storm has been spotted in the vicinity. A storm warning must be initiated.

This "storm warning" means active management: face-to-face interviews with the subject, and/or collateral interviews with family or peers; an in-depth review of records (e.g., military, criminal, residence, police incidents, employment); social media monitoring; possible civil commitment, safety plan development for school, work, home, and the community at large; and obtaining signed consents to communicate with mental health professionals to monitor progress. The U.S. Secret Service employs the TRAP-18 to detect potential threats to the president and other political figures.

It is critical to note that the TRAP-18 is not a predictive test or checklist with which to "profile" individuals. Instead, it is a structured professional judgment tool, akin to a barometric pressure reading for a meteorologist. It advances the hypothesis that the discovery of one proximal warning behavior should trigger active threat management, while the presence of only distal characteristics means the case should simply be monitored. Utilization of the TRAP-18 requires training in the use of structured professional instruments.[1-4]

The concept of "warning behaviors" originates from the work of the Fixated Research Group in the United Kingdom on abnormal communications and approaches to the British royal family[5]; these have been called "pre-attack signals" by other authors.[6] Since a structured approach to interpreting such warning behaviors had been missing from the threat assessment research, they were organized and operationalized after intensive research on targeted or intended violence, discussions with colleagues, and the casework of the original authors. The eight warning behaviors capture behavioral or psychological patterns that indicate change, and that may suggest accelerating risk.[7] They contain dynamic (changeable and changing) rather than static (unchanging) factors because the former are typically more indicative of short-term violence, which is usually the focus of threat assessment.[8] The warning behaviors are not discrete variables, but patterns for analysis[9] based on known and well-studied samples of intended violence including school shooters versus school threateners, intimate partner homicide,[10] and mass murders in Germany and Switzerland.[11] The 18 indicators are classified as either present or absent if there is sufficient evidence to make a determination.

THE EIGHT PROXIMAL WARNING BEHAVIORS

The eight proximal warning behaviors of the TRAP-18 (our "storm warning" of violence) are as follows.[1-4,9,10]

1. *Pathway*: The warning behavior is research, planning, preparation, or implementation of an attack.
2. *Fixation*: The warning behavior indicates an increasingly pathological preoccupation with a person or a cause, accompanied by a deterioration in social and occupational functioning.
    Note: Fixation is distinguished through clinical examination of one of three different cognitive-affective drivers: delusion, obsession, or extreme overvalued belief. Delusions are usually accompanied by other psychotic symptoms, such as visual or auditory hallucinations, grossly disorganized speech (suggesting formal thought disorder), and disorganized behavior. Isolated delusions without the other classic symptoms of schizophrenia or a mood disorder do exist as delusional disorder, but these should also suggest the possibility that the individual has obsessions or, more commonly, extreme overvalued beliefs.[12]
3. *Identification*: The warning behavior indicates a psychological desire to be a pseudo commando, have a warrior mentality, closely associate with weapons or other military or law enforcement paraphernalia, identify with previous attackers or assassins, or identify oneself as an agent to advance a particular cause or belief system.
4. *Novel aggression*: The warning behavior is an act of violence that appears unrelated to any targeted violence pathway and is committed for the first time. It is often a test of one's capability to carry out an act of violence.
5. *Energy burst*: The warning behavior is an increase in the frequency or variety of any noted activities related to the target, even if the activities themselves are relatively innocuous, usually in the hours, days, or weeks before the attack.
6. *Leakage*: The warning behavior is the communication to a third party of an intent to do harm to a target through an attack.[13]

7. *Last resort*: The warning behavior is evidence of a "violent action imperative" and "time imperative"; it is often a signal of desperation or distress.
8. *Directly communicated threat*: The warning behavior is the communication of a direct threat to the target or law enforcement beforehand.

THE 10 DISTAL CHARACTERISTICS OF THE TRAP-18

The 10 distal characteristics of the TRAP-18 (our "storm watch" of violence) are as follows.[1-4,9,10]

1. *Personal grievance and moral outrage* join personal life experience with certain historical, religious, or political events. The personal grievance is often defined by a major loss in love or work, feelings of anger and humiliation, and the blaming of others. Moral outrage is typically the vicarious identification with a group that has suffered (or is perceived to have suffered), even though the individual usually has not experienced the same suffering, if any at all.
2. *Framed by an ideology* is the presence of a belief system that justifies the individual's intent to act. It can be a religious belief system, a political philosophy, a secular commitment, a one-issue conflict, or an idiosyncratic justification.
3. *Failure to affiliate with an extremist or other group* is defined by the actual failure to join, or the rejection of the individual by, a group of which he wants to be part.
4. *Dependence on the virtual community* is evidence of the individual's active communication with others through social media, chat rooms, e-mails, listservs, texting, tweeting, and so forth about his radical or extreme beliefs.
5. *Thwarting of occupational goals* is a major setback or failure in a planned occupational life course.
6. *Changes in thinking and emotion* are indicated when thoughts and their expression become more strident, simplistic, and absolute. Argument ceases and preaching begins. Persuasion yields to imposition of one's beliefs on others. There is no critical analysis of theory or opinion, and the mantra "Do not think, just believe" is adopted. Emotions typically move from anger and argument to contempt and disdain for others' beliefs, to disgust for the outgroup and a willingness to homicidally aggress against them. Violence is cloaked in self-righteousness and the pretense of superior belief. Humor is lost.
7. *Failure of sexually intimate pair bonding* is present if the individual has historically failed to form a lasting sexually intimate relationship.
8. *Mental disorder* is present if there was evidence of a major mental disorder.

9. *Creativity and innovation* are present if there is evidence of tactical thinking "outside the box"; the act being planned has not been done before in contemporaneous times or is likely to be imitated by future offenders.
10. *Criminal violence* is present if there is evidence of instrumental criminal violence by history prior to the act of terrorism (e.g., history of armed robberies or planned assaults).

The TRAP-18 has been subjected to peer-reviewed studies testing its reliability and validity, including research independent of its developer.[14,15] The retrospective nature of the studies and the small sample sizes have to be taken into account when interpreting the results. Further research is needed, and potential weaknesses of the TRAP-18 (e.g., its lack of protective factors) must be considered, but the results so far seem promising.

It is important to note that predatory (planned, calm) and affective (reactive, impulsive, full of adrenaline) violence are different (see Chapter 6 for an example from the JFK assassination). The TRAP-18 is not the only threat assessment instrument in use today. Others used to assess risk of terrorist violence include the ERG 22+[16] and the VERA (Violent Extremism Risk Assessment).[17] More than one approach is considered best for the assessment of terrorism risk, and other instruments that measure violence risk, such as the HCR-20 V3[18] and the PCL-R,[19] are also recommended. Like the TRAP-18, they were developed to help make structured decisions about violence risk.

The application of instruments is only the first step. Threat management can only succeed through an interdisciplinary approach. Law enforcement, forensic, and general mental health professionals and other experts must join forces. We have not elaborated on the prevalence of mental disorders in terrorists, but while some violence may stem from long-held racist attitudes—as is evident in the globalization of the White supremacist movement—other violence is the result of a combination of mental illness and radicalization in the attacker. The potential for human loss is the same, but management strategies to prevent such attacks are quite different (e.g., ensuring medical–psychiatric treatment vs. no treatment). Cases must be analyzed on an individual level since a "one size fits all" strategy is likely doomed to fail.[1,20]

MANAGEMENT OF PATHOLOGICAL FIXATIONS

As far as classifying pathological fixations as delusion, obsession, or extreme overvalued belief, preliminary findings show a high level of agreement between forensic psychiatrists when they are asked to choose among three definitions with fictionalized vignettes. In a study conducted by the *American Academy of Psychiatry and the Law*, forensic psychiatrists were asked to read 12 randomized fictionalized vignettes featuring criminal behavior.[21] They were then asked to select one of three definitions (i.e., obsession, delusion, or extreme overvalued belief) as the motive for the behavior. The study revealed that psychiatrists were able to perform this task well, and with high levels of agreement. As such, cognitive affective drivers of pathological fixations should be identified and then managed or treated utilizing the following guidance.

Delusions

Delusions in the context of a major mental disorder are amenable to treatment with psychotropic medications, and most such patients will benefit from antipsychotic drugs. Current guidelines support the use of antipsychotic drugs in the management of schizophrenia or in mood disorders with psychotic features (e.g., bipolar or unipolar mood disorders). Substance-induced psychotic disorders (e.g., amphetamine) can also appear with quite elaborate hallucinations and delusions. Such individuals may commit acts of serious violence toward others, including law enforcement officers, due to the physiologically arousing and paranoia-inducing properties of the stimulants. Antipsychotic drugs can be beneficial in such cases and may require several weeks or months of treatment in a drug-free environment to clear psychotic symptoms. Subjects with persecutory, religious or atypical psychotic disorders such as Capgras syndrome are considered to be a threat to others, especially if the individual is fearful of being harmed. Capgras delusions are those in which a person believes others, such as loved ones, have been replaced by an imposter (e.g., "I know that is not my real mother because she does not talk or walk like that"). Such encapsulated delusions in the absence of other symptoms are more difficult to treat. Psychiatrists are taught to remain neutral to delusional content (i.e., not challenging their veracity), which allows them to establish trust and better rapport, where such engagement is vital to treatment.[12,22]

Example: A 38-year-old woman is arrested after she threatens to stab and kill her gynecologist. She believes that the doctor is trying to kill her unborn baby by forcibly performing an abortion on her. She is taken to an emergency room after her arrest because the police cannot understand her speech patterns and she is so upset about her "unborn baby being harmed." A pregnancy test is found to be negative, yet she insists that she is carrying "the Son of God" in her body. She can hear voices of many gods and demons telling her she is a bad person who must stop her doctor from killing her unborn baby. On examination she is disheveled and has grossly disorganized speech. She is civilly committed and prescribed a long-acting injectable antipsychotic drug.

Obsessions

Obsessions in a forensic or threat-assessment context, fixations driven by obsessional thoughts, are very infrequent and generally do not pose a risk of violence. However, there is a limited body of research reaching back to the early 20th century wherein such violent behaviors were called *catathymic homicides*.[23]

Texas clock tower sniper Charles Whitman (who had a brain tumor), discussed in Chapter 2, may have been motivated by obsessions.[12]

Example: A 25-year-old woman is seen by police after she tells her neighbor that she has thoughts of stabbing her family. She is visibly upset when evaluated and states that she loves her family and would never want them harmed by anyone. She reports images of seeing her siblings being stabbed that will not leave her mind. She tries to distract herself by singing or walking around. By the end of the interview, she is calmer and feels her thoughts are "silly" but very intrusive. She has some low mood and insomnia but denies all other symptoms and is willing to seek help for this problem. She is prescribed an antidepressant that is also indicated for obsessive-compulsive disorder and provided cognitive behavioral therapy.

Extreme Overvalued Beliefs

There is no known evidence-based mental health treatment for a lone offender with extreme overvalued beliefs (EOBs). The best current data come from established treatment strategies of other disorders characterized by overvalued ideas, such as eating disorders, parasitophobia (Ekbom's syndrome), and other paranoid states. Psychiatric inpatients with eating disorders have a high incident of co-occurring mental disorders. In one study, 69% met criteria for at least one personality disorder diagnosis and up to 93% also experienced substance abuse, anxiety, and depression (which are all treatable). Such co-occurring disorders worsen the prognosis and behavioral events in eating disorders[24] (see Chapter 6). Similar findings of mental disorders are found in lone-actor terrorism studies.[25] Therefore, individuals presenting with EOBs in threat management should be screened and treated for similar disorders. Conspiracy theories, spirited religious fervor, or political ideology can grow rapidly, as the user sees more content without counterbalancing information. This is partially a result of today's social media algorithms, which filter content according to one's interests or "likes." This process of fixating on ideas may later coalesce into a self-identity or identification.[12] Recent research suggests that such an evolution, from fixation to identification, may be an indicator of mobilization for violence. Likewise, over time, individuals with an eating disorder change their diets so radically that cognitive shortcuts allow them to act without thinking each time they encounter food. The fixation "food will make me fat" becomes the identification "I am fat." For the lone-actor terrorist, the fixation "I believe in the authority of the U.S. Constitution" becomes the identification "It is 1776, the U.S. Capitol belongs to US, and we are taking it back." The paradox is that the professional involved will usually never know whether the (terrorist) act would have occurred if he or she had not intervened. Nevertheless, the need to focus upon fact-based, dynamic behaviors in the present, rather than static diagnoses or historical factors, is the key to successful prevention.[1]

Example: A woman overhears her 43-year-old husband's plans to kill a police officer during a routine traffic stop because he believes that he is not answerable to any government statutes, including paying taxes. She stops him from accessing his gun. A police investigation later reveals that he formed many odd beliefs after several years of internet use. It is determined that he and others he interacted with online believe that the U.S. government was originally set up by the founding fathers but was secretly replaced by a new government system based on admiralty law, the law of the sea, and international commerce. He tells his mental health team that he is a member of the sovereign citizen movement. On evaluation, he spent much time talking about his redemption ideas, admitted to heavy alcohol use, and also discussed childhood abuse at the hands of his father. He begins to trust his therapist and is prescribed naltrexone for alcohol cravings.

It should be pointed out here that it is possible for a case to have more than one cognitive affective driver—making these difficult to tease apart.[26] Consider the terrorist Tobias Rathjen in Hanau, Germany. He stated that he was guided by voices, and that he was under the control of "intelligence agency mind readers." On February 19, 2020, he killed nine individuals with migrant backgrounds before murdering his mother and taking his own life. He not only had a history of schizophrenia, but also right-wing extremist beliefs. Using the TRAP-18, researchers recently described a complex interplay of delusions, obsessions, and EOBs to explain Rathjen's motivation for the attack. While most cases of targeted attacks involve EOBs, those with more than one type of fixation could also pose a challenge for the legal system in determining criminal culpability.

5

Anorexia Nervosa, Querulants, and Others

The patient, who was a plump, healthy girl until the beginning of last year (1887), began, early in February, without apparent cause, to evince a repugnance to food; and soon afterwards declined to take any whatever, except half a cup of tea or coffee.[1]

—SIR WILLIAM GULL, M.D.

"You can't be too rich or too thin." While the origins of this popular expression are a subject of debate, its implications are clear, and serve as a subcultural mantra for millions of people.[2] The notion that you can never be *too* thin is extreme, overvalued, and shared, arousing deep concerns in family and friends, and with good reason. Individuals with eating disorders have significantly elevated mortality rates, often due to suicide, with the highest rates of death occurring in those with anorexia nervosa.[3] Despite numerous studies, no specific genes or brain defects have thus far been identified as causing eating disorders, which points instead to the importance of psychological contributions to this disorder.[4,5]

Anorexia *hysterique* (later renamed anorexia *nervosa*) was first described by Sir William Gull (1816–1890), court physician to the Prince of Wales and Queen Victoria, and French psychiatrist Ernst-Charles Lasègue (1816–1883). Gull, observing that the problem was mostly found in girls and young women aged 16 to 23 years old, recognized its important psychological origins, and described the disorder as an "ego perversion" in an 1888 publication.[1] Several British texts, including Sims's *Symptoms in the Mind*,[6] considered by many students in the United Kingdom as the definitive descriptive guidebook for psychopathology, identify anorexia nervosa as a disorder of overvalued ideas.[7]

As we will later explore, Sims's guide also categorizes querulous (litigious) paranoid state, morbid jealousy, parasitophobia (fixation on the idea that one is infested with parasites), and dysmorphophobia (body dysmorphic disorder) as disorders characterized by overvalued ideas.[6] Though they have a similar cognitive-affective driver, they differ widely in their content—but the result is the same: the individual is driven toward a single cause, seemingly blind to everything else. The belief is increasingly relished, amplified, and defended, alongside an accompanying intense emotional commitment—in the case of anorexia, to losing weight. The belief in question becomes "an acceptable, comprehensible idea by the patient beyond the bounds of reason" and causes "disturbed function or suffering to the person himself or others."[6(p132)] Sims's guide analogizes the behavior as being carried out "with the drive of an instinct, like nest building."[6(p132)] Today these disorders are often fueled by online interactions, for instance through pro–eating disorder websites and social media groups.

Anorexia is nothing new, likely subject in part to fashion trends and shifting standards of beauty through the centuries.[8] What is new, however, is the ease with which those with the disorder can subscribe to the group mentality of many like minds gathered together online—and without countering viewpoints. Peer and media effects are well known to contribute to eating disorder behaviors by intensifying previously held rigid beliefs about weight and eating. Online eating disorder subcultures in the United States have been shown to worsen disordered behavior by intensifying beliefs regarding appearance and weight; indeed, the app Instagram is accused of propagating eating disorder deaths as well as suicides in new lawsuits—highlighting the online contagion effect.[9] In a Stanford University study of nearly 700 American families with a child diagnosed with an eating disorder, 35.5% of those young people visited pro–eating disorder sites—and among those, 96.0% reported learning new weight loss or purging techniques. The authors concluded in their paper, "Surfing for Thinness," that pro–eating disorder website visits were prevalent among adolescents with eating disorders and that their parents had little knowledge of this.[10]

With faddish intensity, variations in various disorders involving appearance, weight, and physical attributes are categorized by psychiatrists as distinct disorders: anorexia nervosa, bulimia nervosa, binge eating disorder, purging disorder, avoidant/restrictive food intake disorder, body dysmorphic disorder, and now orthorexia (fixation on eating healthy) and bigorexia (extreme body building). Importantly, many diagnosed with these disorders have co-occurring mood, anxiety, and substance use disorders, obsessive-compulsive disorder, and/or suicidal thoughts. These comorbid conditions may also dampen higher brain functioning, allowing cognitive shortcuts to develop into pathological fixations.[11] As noted earlier, a person may easily transition from the fixation "food will make me fat" to the more harmful personal identification, "I am a fat person."[12] Though anorexia can be lethal, certain treatments may be life-saving, including group therapy and providing a structured routine of eating with others. Online applications of such positive group effects are worthy of future study.

The fact that harm to oneself through starvation can occur as a result of these overvalued ideas is well known to psychiatrists who have civilly committed people with anorexia nervosa in order to provide them with sustenance essential to their survival. Dangerously ill and underweight people may passionately defend their cases with intense emotional commitments to calorie avoidance and exercise. At the same time, it is important to note that people with anorexia are no more likely than those without it to engage in violent behavior—their actions are threats to their own safety and well-being, not to others'.

BODY DYSMORPHIC DISORDER

One of the more curious examples of overvalued ideas as they relate to eating and body image, body dysmorphic disorder (BDD), involves the conviction that some body part is hopelessly flawed, malformed, or ugly. Those with this disorder may check the mirror many times a day looking for any sign of improvement, or they may avoid mirrors and socializing completely. More often than not, people with BDD suffer in silence. While most of us are dissatisfied with one or more of our own physical attributes, those with BDD have an extreme preoccupation with an "imagined" defect in their appearance which interferes markedly with their quality of life. The face or body part in question varies from person to person, with skin being the most prevalent source of concern, followed by hair, nose, eyes, legs/knees, chin/jaw, breasts, stomach/waist, and lips. People with BDD often see problems with more than just one aspect of their appearance. Such individuals are often socially isolated, depressed, and at higher risk of committing suicide. Approximately 80% of individuals with body dysmorphic disorder have experienced suicidal thoughts, and 24% to 28% attempt suicide.[13-16]

In her book on the subject, *The Broken Mirror*, psychiatrist Katherine Phillips mentions that people who have BDD focus on "defects" that others consider minimal or don't see at all.[16] Yet the suffering endured by those with BDD is palpable, and often includes an intense emotional commitment for their grievance to be heard and validated—through relentless pursuit of cosmetic procedures. They might continuously seek surgery for a perceived crooked nose or smaller lips, often with dismaying aesthetic results. The procedures often fail to reduce the severity of their pathological fixations.

Phillips has been able to trace cases of body dysmorphic disorder back a century or more. It was first described by Italian psychiatrist Enrico Moreselli in 1886. According to Phillips, about 40% of patients are concerned with a single body part over the course of the disorder. Roughly the same number applies to sufferers who begin concerned with one body part and then adopt others over time. One patient, for instance, initially worried about his ears, but later exhibited extreme concern over a crooked lip, and then a scar on his neck. All three ultimately came into play at once.[16]

Another less common pattern may emerge when specific concerns are less consistent. A person may be concerned about their nose for a while, but then shift focus to their eyes or hair. One fixation ends and a new one begins. Current American guides describe BDD as being characterized by delusional or obsessional beliefs.[13] However, variants of this disorder have also been described by

British investigators as overvalued ideas,[6] in which an individual has a passionate fixation and relishes, amplifies, and defends the desire to have a better body part.

QUERULANTS

Any sitting judge will attest that the court system today is overrun with "frivolous" lawsuits. But sometimes legal action *in extremis* comes into play with a plaintiff who can be convinced of nothing other than the rightness and ultimate justification of his case, blind to all else. When this behavior reaches pathological levels, such individuals are known as vexatious litigators or *querulants*. Swiss-German psychiatrist Karl Jaspers described querulants in his textbook *Allgemeine Psychopathologie* (General Psychopathology),[17] wherein he argues that such variations of human nature (frustrating and potentially dangerous as they may be, I would add) should not be classified as mental illness.

Instead, Jaspers described the fixation seen in querulants as part of an abnormal personality structure:

> the fanatic who devotes himself wholly to a single cause and is blind to everything else. He does this so unconditionally that he will unconsciously risk his whole existence on its behalf. Credulous belief, the exaggeration of some isolated purpose out of all context is the special interest of their existence. They are driven, harried people who get a specific and agonist pleasure from their identification with some solitary cause. Kurt Schneider differentiates the "combative fanatic" (aggressive fanatic) from the damped-down or more reserved fanatic. The former will assert their rights or supposed rights and are "querulants." The latter merely tend to demonstrate and nurse their convictions. They are born sectarians, cranks and representatives of esoteric doctrines for which they live with an inner self-assurance and proud contempt of everyone else.[17(p441)]

Contempt, along with anger and disgust, have recently also been identified as important emotions in intergroup aggression and political violence (see Chapter 9).

Stephen White, a psychologist and threat assessment researcher, frequently consults with public and private organizations and with academic institutions on cases involving subjects who come to attention due to communicated threats, bizarre presentations, and/or increasing agitation and desperation.[18] According to Dr. White, a difficult scenario facing threat-management teams and legal departments is the "vexatious litigant" or whistle-blower run amok—highlighting the need for corroborating claims. In these cases, a complaint at first may seem valid—perhaps a company appears to be putting its staff or customers at risk; there are many such cases in which the accusation is legitimate. But in the case of the vexatious litigant, it slowly becomes apparent that the individual is on a hollow, self-aggrandizing quest to harass the powerful and prominent with spurious petitions and pleas. They often develop a grievance, feel persecuted, and self-identify as fighting "forces of corruption." These individuals raise concerns about violence risk given their fixations, demands to be recognized, and increasingly grandiose lists of complaints and accompanying insults. On rare occasions these cases culminate in violence committed against perceived persecutors and other obstructionists to their cases.

According to Australian psychiatrists Paul E. Mullen and Grant Lester, the term *querulous* itself (from the Latin for plaintive murmuring) describes a pattern of behavior involving the unusually persistent pursuit of a personal grievance in a manner seriously damaging to the individual's own economic, social, and personal interests, and disruptive to the functioning of the courts and/or other agencies involved in addressing their claims.[19]

In civil cases, attorneys, judges, and mental health professionals frequently encounter clients who complain to an abnormal degree about an individual or a company. They will often seek compensation or retribution for a grievance by utilizing the legal system, often as a *pro se* litigant (appearing for oneself and not retaining an attorney). Western legal practice holds the view that everyone has a moral right to pursue and rectify a wrong—a shared cultural belief that some would consider to be particularly American; however, the relentless pursuit of a claim with little or no merit can be relished, amplified, and defended by a litigant, creating chaos for judges, law clerks, and defendants. Claims are often devoid of logical constraint and may include long lists of grievances: defective equipment, medical malpractice, exposure to toxic substances such as asbestos, radon, mold, second-hand smoke; bugs, bias, harassment, fraud, and so on. The fixations grow more dominant over time, more refined, and more resistant to challenge. The individual nurtures an intense emotional commitment to the grievance and may continue to pursue trivial, unfounded lawsuits—often claiming that judges and the system itself are corrupt. Claims are often backed by "research" the individual has conducted, relying on online subcultures to "prove" their case. Such tenacious persistence can lead to the querulant's own financial collapse and/or escalate to violent behavior.[19–21]

Prior to Jaspers, the term *paranoia querulants* was used to explain an excessive urge to challenge authorities, file lawsuits, and/or litigate.[17,20] Notably, Emil Kraepelin (1856–1926) described the mindset of individuals suffering from querulous paranoia in his 1895 article, *Ueber den Querulantenwahnsinn*:

> It appears especially in these patients' total inaccessibility to reason. Even the most obvious evidence does not impress them at all; it is not even deemed worthy of examination. Certainly the patients calmly listen to the arguments addressed to them, admit all that, in their opinion, is harmless but evade every logical constraint by simply repeating previous views or by dealing with all objections using totally inconclusive counter-evidence: "I stick to the point; what is written is written."[20(p336)]

Kraeplin goes on to describe that while in some cases these individuals are delusional, "sane persons may also be querulous under certain conditions and even show obstinacy and passion."[20(p341)] It is striking that Kraeplin (1895) and Wernicke (1892) described observations of rigidly held, non-delusional beliefs within three years of each other, even using the word *Ueber* to emphasize that the beliefs were excessive or extreme, and not always caused by a severe mental illness.

Many querulants have been reported to exhibit oddities in their written communications, such as curious formatting, voluminous pages, strange and irrelevant attachments, as well as colored highlighting, underlining, and unnecessary capitalization.[19,21] An example can be seen in a 2021 case filed in federal court in which a plaintiff alleged damages of $33 million against a religious foundation called Saint Germain. In response to a court order to dismiss the case, the plaintiff passionately persists, writing (oddities preserved):

> I, ___ am an American-born Free on this Land and Soil. I am protected by the Original Constitution for the United States of America of 1776. I have the right to a trial by jury to bring all America the truth. . . .[22(p2–3)]
>
> AMerIca, the ["I AM Race"] is made up of Living, Breathing, Self-Governing inheritors of the Kingdom of the "Mighty 'I AM' Presence." We are the Government, the inheritors of this Kingdom, the "LAND AND SOIL." The Defendants have used malicious force and willful intent to remove our lawful schools. The "I AM" Race is destined to bring peace back to earth as it was intended from the beginning.[22(p3)]

As this text illustrates, the querulous discourse is often rambling and characterized by the misuse of legal or technical terms and may include threats. The querulous provide detailed and apparently logical accounts of the emergence of their grievances and the progress of their quest for justice. The enthusiasm and passionate engagement in their quest for supposed justice can obscure the absurdity of the querulant's expectations and divert attention from the chaos the pursuit has wrought for them and those around them.[23–25]

Academic interest in "querulous paranoia" has declined dramatically in recent years, according to forensic psychiatrist professor Paul E. Mullen, who has extensively studied it, despite the fact that "a proliferation of complaint organizations and agencies of accountability were drawing more and more people into asserting their individual rights through the pursuit of claims and grievances. Querulous behavior, as a result, far from declining, is on the increase, bringing with it suffering for the querulous and disruption to the organizations through which they seek their vision of justice."[24,25]

In an attempt to further examine neglected querulant behavior, Dr. Mullen and his collaborators broke down its severity into three categories:

- *Unusually persistent complainants* who consume time resources through grievances that are, if not downright trivial, lacking in the import that might justify lengthy, concentrated campaigns;
- *Vexatious litigants* who pursue their grievances primarily through the courts;

- *Unusually persistent petitioners* who operate primarily through petitioning prominent people such as politicians and heads of state.[23,24]

Further, a study of 52 unusually persistent complainants suggested that compared to a matched control group, they pursued their complaints far longer and produced far greater volumes of material in support of their cases; nevertheless, their cases were closed having achieved nothing approaching a mutually acceptable resolution.[23-25]

Threats are a frequent accompaniment of querulous behavior. Serious violence may be uncommon, but when it occurs it is often preceded by a period of threatening communications. The group described next is emblematic of what can happen when intractable, even bizarre beliefs are carried too far.

SOVEREIGN CITIZENS

On May 20, 2010, police officers pulled over a white van during a routine traffic stop. Jerry Kane and his 16-year-old son Joseph were the occupants. As officers questioned Jerry, his son unexpectedly stormed out of the minivan and began shooting at the officers with an AK-47 rifle. He shot and killed both, leaving one by the side of the road and the other in ditch. Eventually the two were surrounded in a large Wal-Mart parking lot. A firefight ensued, resulting in the death of the pair. An investigation revealed that they were followers of an anti-government movement known as Sovereign Citizens.

Often described as a cult, Sovereign Citizens are a proud, loosely affiliated group that believe that the U.S. government is illegitimate.[26-30] In 2013, law enforcement ranked Sovereign Citizens as one of the gravest threats to the safety of uniformed officers.[28] Anti-government extremists who claim to be above the law, they attribute their authority to *Posse Comitatus* (Latin for "power of the county"), which in common law means that ordinary people should suppress "lawlessness" to defend the country. The group's history can be traced back to tax protestors and militias.

There are an estimated 300,000 to 500,000 Sovereign Citizens in the United States. They often put together biblical passages, commercial law, admiralty law, and the U.S. Constitution to bolster their extreme overvalued beliefs. Followers of this movement are often contemptuous White, middle-aged men who refuse to pay taxes and believe that they are immune from government authority. Participants may allege that a secret fund is created for everyone at birth, and that a procedure exists to "redeem" or reclaim this money (redemption theory). They cite obscure and outdated laws in order to prove that they cannot be subjected to state or federal law. For instance, they argue that when the United States created the District of Columbia in 1871, it ceased to be a country and became a corporation, because the words "United States of America" appeared in the legislation in all capital letters. According to their reinterpretation of the law, only the names of corporations can be spelled out in all capital letters.[26-30] Sovereign citizens also believe that Franklin D. Roosevelt sold the country to investors in 1933 when he ended the gold standard and "illegally changed" the date of the presidential inauguration from March 4 to January 20.

An offshoot is a group of African Americans identifying themselves as Moorish-American Sovereign Citizens, who also regard themselves as having a privileged legal status, who adhere to redemption theory, and who may misuse liens and create false accounts.

Interestingly, certain members of QAnon have absorbed some of the Sovereigns' assertions into their own philosophies. QAnon members believe that a secret cabal of Satanist, child-eating elites run the United States. Some believed that Joe Biden would be sworn in as the president of the U.S. "corporation," but that Trump would return to office as the president of the *actual* government of the United States.[29-31]

George F. Parker, a forensic psychiatrist at Indiana University Medical School, conducted extensive research on Sovereign Citizens, including the publication of a case series from case files. He observed that Sovereign Citizen defendants support a variety of idiosyncratic legal theories and political beliefs that on the surface appear to be delusional. He concluded that individuals with such beliefs likely have the capacity to understand the nature and objectives of criminal proceedings, and are able to assist their attorneys; therefore, they are competent to stand trial.[30] As such Sovereign Citizen beliefs are not obsessional or delusional in nature. Instead, they are passionately held beliefs shared by others as part of a broader subculture. The beliefs are relished, amplified, and defended by individuals who may carry out violent behavior in their service.[12,30]

VIOLENT GRIEVANCES

A Pennsylvania woman charged in the U.S. Capitol attack of January 6, 2021, demanded that Nancy Pelosi be brought out and hanged. Pauline Bauer, 54 years old, represented herself in court and announced that she was a Sovereign Citizen and that the court had "no power" over her. She objected to being called a person, saying she was "the Living Soul, A Creation of God, A Woman, As One of We the People," and called for "all charges against my VESSEL" to be dropped, according to court documents. Bauer filed a motion to dismiss the criminal case, saying "inconsistencies with Due Process Protections Act and obligations not met under the Brady Rule" mean the charges should be dropped. Her motion was denied.[31]

In the worst mass shooting of recent history, Stephen Paddock fired over 1,000 rounds into the audience of a country music festival, killing 60 and wounding 867 from his sniper's perch at the Mandalay Hotel in Las Vegas. Paddock eventually shot himself, and his motive remains a mystery. His primary EOBs were likely infamy as well as a desire to "outperform" his father, who was once on the "elite" FBI's Most Wanted list for bank robbery.[31-36] Paddock had no prior criminal record or ties to terrorist organizations and was described as narcissistic by his brother. An autopsy found nothing unusual with his brain.[36] He was angry about the way casinos treated wealthy clients. Interestingly, he had filed a lawsuit against the Cosmopolitan of Las Vegas Hotel (about a mile and a half from the Mandalay) after a slip and fall accident due to the "dangerous condition" he claimed the hotel had created.[32] The arbitrator in the case decided Paddock had failed to prove negligence. Despite having significant wealth, Paddock never paid the $270 in court fees, indicating he may have also held an overvalued grievance regarding the outcome of his case. Paddock booked two rooms at the Chicago Blackstone Hotel overlooking the Lollapalooza Festival two months prior to the Las Vegas attack. The Mandalay Bay, the Cosmopolitan Hotel, and several other casinos were owned by the Blackstone Group.[31-36]

6

Lee Harvey Oswald

A New Perspective

I'm just a Patsy.

—Lee Harvey Oswald

One of the most analyzed and documented acts of violence in American history is likely the assassination of President John F. Kennedy in November 1963. While conspiracy theories still abound, the conclusion drawn in the Warren Commission report, that assassin Lee Harvey Oswald was the sole perpetrator of the crime, has to a large degree been accepted as true by experts who have closely examined all the available evidence. Even so, a 2013 Gallup poll found that only 30% of Americans believed that Oswald acted alone, with many pointing to the Mafia or federal government as potential conspirators.[1] Today, modern forensic definitions and threat assessment tools allow us to review Oswald's case in a different light.

Unfortunately, no interview of Oswald was conducted by a forensic psychiatrist after his arrest. Modern criteria for mental illnesses as defined in the *Diagnostic and Statistical Manual of Mental Disorders*[2] had not yet been developed in 1963, leaving Oswald's mental state at the time of the assassination an open question. Past psychological analyses have suggested that he was certainly "capable of murder."[3] Studies in recent years indicate that most acts of targeted violence are not perpetrated by psychotic (delusional) individuals, but instead by those with extreme overvalued beliefs (EOBs).[4,5]

The proximal warning behaviors and distal characteristics of lone-actor terrorists developed by Reid Meloy (the Terrorist Radicalization and Assessment Protocol, or TRAP-18, discussed in Chapter 3), are now widely used to assess risk.[6,7] But in my role as an associate professor at a prominent medical school, I find that vivid examples from history are often useful to illustrate key points. There is always bias when a case is reviewed retrospectively, but I was interested in the role that EOBs might have had in the JFK assassination. As such, in this chapter I will, for the first time, contend that Lee Harvey Oswald exhibited five proximal warning signs and eight distal characteristics of lone-actor terrorism. Utilizing the vast body of information that is now known about Oswald, I aim to explore whether his mental state (based in part upon a 1953 psychiatric report) and other conditions align with the official narrative that he acted alone. I will discuss whether Oswald's proximal warning signs and distal characteristics could have alerted authorities to a possible lone-actor terrorist threat. The aim here is to analyze whether threat-assessment tools could have identified Oswald as a potential threat to the president, thus placing him on the radar for the U.S. Secret Service. This analysis, I hope, will also provide a useful teaching case for application of the TRAP-18,[6,7] which has been applied to other protective intelligence cases, including that of Sirhan Bishara Sirhan, who shot and killed Robert F. Kennedy in 1968.[7] The circumstances surrounding the JFK assassination will likely continue to be a source of popular speculation and disagreement, but I have tried my best to achieve factual clarity regarding Oswald's mental state at the time of the assassination.

OSWALD'S SELF-INJURIOUS BEHAVIORS

The body of Lee Harvey Oswald was examined during an autopsy on November 24, 1963. Just hours earlier, Oswald had been awaiting charges for his role in the alleged assassination of President Kennedy. Oswald, now cooling down but not yet in rigor mortis, was 5 feet 9 inches tall, and weighed 150 pounds. He had a massive gunshot wound to his abdomen, resulting in a severe hemorrhage from aortic and other vessel tears. He had a 1¼ inch vertical scar with cross hatching on his left arm, a remnant from prior self-injurious cutting behavior that had required sutures. He also had a puckered and irregular scar below his left deltoid from another old wound—an "accidental" gunshot sustained when he was in the Marines. Outwardly appearing to be a stable, married man, the scars instead epitomized Oswald's long history of character and temperamental problems resulting in tumultuous work, military, and social issues. According to his own diary, on October 21, 1959, Oswald was found bleeding and unconscious in a Russian hotel room bathtub after he had slashed his wrist. He was taken to a hospital where he received sutures, resulting in the tell-tale cross hatching seen during this autopsy.[8-10]

A self-described Marxist-Leninist, Oswald expected fame and notoriety when he defected to the Soviet Unionin the late 1950s, but the KGB became highly suspicious of him and turned him away. He was distraught after being told that he could no longer remain in the Communist country. A former KGB deputy chief who defected to the United States in 1964 told FBI agents that Oswald would have died if the hotel manager had not broken down the door to save his life.[9-11]

The gunshot wound scar was thought to be the result of "accidentally dropping" a Derringer 0.22 pistol that Oswald kept in his locker when he was in the Marines.

Apparently, he was alone in his cubicle when a gunshot was heard. He calmly told another Marine, "I believe I shot myself."[9(p554)] Some of his fellow Marines believed he had *purposely* shot himself in order to stay in the Japanese town where he was stationed, rather than leaving for the Philippines with his unit. In a separate incident, a fellow Marine claimed that Oswald had staged a scene in which he had fired several shots at mysterious "men in the woods," and was found slumped against a tree while shaking and crying. Oswald stated that he could not bear doing guard duty and was sent back to Japan for "medical treatment."[9(p558)]

Self-inflicted injury is a common problem encountered in psychiatry. It can sometimes be associated with unstable personality, mood disorders, and/or psychosis or substance use disorders. In the case of maladaptive personality traits, such individuals can be manipulative and have a high level of negative affect. They may also have had an unstable upbringing characterized by attachment difficulties (insecure bonds with caregivers), often with poor childhood emotional nurturance. The physical scars noted during Oswald's autopsy were a record, I would argue, of a series of adulthood defeats and failures in work.[3] Seen through this lens, it is not surprising that Oswald would later claim to be a "patsy" and dismiss the photo of him holding the rifle with which he shot Kennedy as a "fake." Oswald was an expert on how to deceive others, how to game the system to his advantage. Kennedy's visit to Dallas in the fall of 1963 would offer Oswald an extraordinary opportunity to act upon the biggest stage imaginable, to be truly *special*.

OSWALD'S EXTREME OVERVALUED BELIEFS

As seen with many other lone-actor terrorists motivated by EOBs,[4] such as Dylan Roof (the white supremacist) or Malik Hassan (the Fort Hood shooter), Lee Harvey Oswald held EOBs of a Marxist-Leninist philosophical nature. He believed that he would one day become an important historical figure. His beliefs were commonly espoused by others in 1960s leftist subculture. Indeed, music legend Bob Dylan, just weeks after Kennedy's death, announced to a New York Civil Liberties audience, "I've got to admit that the man who shot President Kennedy, Lee Oswald, I don't know exactly where—what he thought he was doing, but I got to admit honestly that I too—I saw some of myself in him. I don't think it would have gone—I don't think it could go that far. But I got to stand up and say I saw things that he felt, in me—not to go that far and shoot."[12(np)] Dylan's comments were widely rebuked, and he later apologized for them.

Oswald relished, amplified, and defended his extreme political philosophy throughout much of his adult life. In *Reclaiming History*,[9] author and former L.A. County District Attorney Vincent Bugliosi gives a detailed account of Oswald's beliefs as elicited by Secret Service inspector Thomas J. Kelley during his interrogation. In the interview, Oswald portrayed Karl Marx as his "religion" and claimed to be a student of philosophy, stating that he did not consider even the Bible to be "a reasonable or intelligent philosophy."[9(p261)]

Oswald's EOBs, like those of many lone-actor terrorists, were refined over time, becoming more dominant and more resistant to challenge. At age 13 he was handed a pamphlet by an older woman advocating for Julius and Ethel Rosenberg, who were convicted of passing U.S. atomic secrets to the Soviet Union. Bugliosi writes, "While it's too much to assume that a single pamphlet turned a thirteen-year-old into a committed Marxist, Lee has probably found a metaphor for the outward expression of his dissatisfaction with life, for the rage of a child who believed he had been abused and neglected, not only by his mother but also by the schools, the courts, the entire system."[9(p539–40)] His psychiatrist noted his limited repertoire of interests at age 13, and his wife would later tell investigators about his philosophical and grandiose fixations.[8–10] The seeds of moral outrage and personal grievance began to take root.

Since there are a plethora of conspiracy theories regarding the Kennedy assassination, it can be difficult to separate accurate information from everything else. Therefore, for the following sections on proximal warning signs and distal characteristics,[6,7] I consulted author and investigative journalist Gerald Posner.[10,11] His book, *Case Closed: Lee Harvey Oswald and the Assassination of JFK*,[10] strongly endorses the official Warren Commission's finding[9] that Oswald acted alone through clear evidentiary detail. A closer look at Oswald's ideology helps us understand his desire to carry out violent acts in the service of his EOBs.

It is clear that Oswald did not suffer from a psychotic mental illness (there is no evidence of hallucinations, delusions, or grossly disorganized speech and behavior).[3] Instead, seen through the lens of EOBs, Oswald's motives are strikingly similar to those of other lone-actor terrorists such as Dylann Roof, the neo-Nazi killer of nine in a historically Black church who wrote, "I hate the sight of the American flag. Modern American patriotism is an absolute joke."[13(p 67)] Each despised different aspects of America and were seeking notoriety within their unique subcultures. Roof wanted to lead the start of a race war. Oswald's motive was a perverted form of Marxism, which he thought would make him famous. At a time when most Americans opposed the Fidel Castro regime in Cuba, Oswald was passing out pro-Castro leaflets reading, "Hands Off," and "Fair Play" for Cuba.[9,10,13,14]

Delusions are beliefs that are idiosyncratic and not shared by others.[4] Oswald's beliefs, while unpopular, were certainly shared by others in his 1960s Leftist subculture, which brought attention to the plight of the common worker and passionately defended its Marxist views—including prominent intellectuals of the time. A notable group of authors and academic scholars were listed as sponsors of a *Fair Play for Cuba* advertisement, including Truman Capote, Norman Mailer, James Baldwin, Simone de Beauvoir, Dan Wakefield, and others.[9] Ironically, Norman Mailer, author of *Oswald's Tale*,[15] concludes that Oswald assassinated Kennedy in service of his ideology and grandiose ambitions. The *shared* nature of EOBs is important in differentiating them from delusions and obsessions.[4,14] Though most literary celebrities were not willing to commit violent acts, many sympathized with Oswald's Cuban Leftist political ideology prior to 1963.[9,12]

WARNING SIGNS MISSED

Lone-actor violence such as assassinations are not impulsive and typically are not a reaction to imminent threats. Oswald's violent actions were not reactional and impulsive, but instead were predatory and intentional. Applying the Terrorist Radicalization and Assessment Protocol (TRAP-18)[6,7] discussed earlier to Oswald[11] yields five *proximal warning behaviors*: pathway, fixation, identification, novel aggression, and last resort. Recall from Chapter 3 that only one is needed to escalate from a "watch" status of sorts to a "warning" status. However, not all of these conditions were known to the FBI prior to the assassination. There were also eight of the TRAP-18's *distal characteristics* of Oswald's behavior at the time: personal grievance and moral outrage, framed by an ideology, failure to affiliate with an extremist or other group, thwarting of occupational goals, changes in thinking and emotion, mental disorder, creativity and innovation, and criminal violence.[7,11]

Oswald's five proximal warnings behaviors are as follows.

1. *Fixation* is an increasingly pathological preoccupation with a person or a cause, accompanied by a deterioration in social and/or occupational life.[6] As a teenager, Oswald discovered socialist literature. As an adult he subscribed to *The Militant*, which describes itself as a "Socialist newsweekly published in the interests of working people." Just 20 days before the assassination, *The Militant* published an article about Cuba, "Lift the Blockade," which accused the Kennedy administration, with its bungled Bay of Pigs invasion, of being "hypocrites." With an almost religious fervor, Oswald had already been proselytizing his political beliefs by distributing "Fair Play for Cuba" leaflets in New Orleans (though not a single person took one). Oswald's Russian wife, Marina, claimed that he had a "sick imagination," adding, "He was very much interested, exceedingly so, in autobiographical works of outstanding statesmen of the United States and elsewhere. I think he compared himself to those people whose autobiographies he read."[8-10,14] Such grandiose self-importance is often seen in lone-actor terrorists that move from fixation to *identification* with/as an important historical figure or martyr.
2. *Identification* in this context is a psychological desire to be a "pseudo-commando" or to have a warrior mentality; to closely associate with weapons or other military or law enforcement paraphernalia; to identify with previous attackers or assassins; or to identify oneself as an agent to advance a particular cause or belief system.[7] For example, only six months before he perpetrated the mass shooting at Parkland's Marjorie Douglas High school, Nikolas Cruz posted to social media the words, "I'm going to be a professional school shooter." Lone-actor attackers will also often photograph or videotape themselves with weapons.[7] Oswald regarded himself as destined to change the course of human

events. The day after Kennedy's death, police discovered the famous photo of Oswald holding the murder weapon. This is a textbook example of the *identification* warning behavior.[7] Oswald had asked Marina to photograph him holding the Mannlicher-Carcano rifle that he used to shoot President Kennedy (and which he had used earlier in the attempted assassination of General Edwin Walker). At the time (April 1963), Oswald was working for a photography plant in Dallas, and he used the last day as an opportunity to get large prints made of himself holding the rifle. Police found copies of the photograph and two negatives. Oswald autographed the photo for a friend, adding the date in Russian style: "To my friend George from Lee Oswald., 5/IV/63." On the back of the photo Marina wrote, in a mocking fashion, "Hunter after Fascists, ha ha ha."[8] Evidently, she had noticed his fascination and identification as a warrior/hunter for his Leftist cause. Oswald later lied to detectives, stating he had never seen the photo before and suggesting that it had been doctored. Conspiracy theorists have claimed it is a forgery, even though experts have conclusively proven they were taken with Oswald's camera, and that the handwriting on the photo was indeed his.[9,10]

Similar to beliefs espoused in manifestos or statements made by other lone-actor terrorists, Oswald's beliefs were refined over time to form his own grandiose philosophy, selectively assembled from various Leftist sources. Norman Mailer in *Oswald's Tale*[15] sums up the assassin's overvalued fixations, "he was above Capitalism, he was above Communism. Both! He had, as he would have seen it, a superior dedication, and the potential of a man like Lenin."[15(p780)]

3. *Pathway* refers to research, planning, preparation for, and/or implementation of an attack.[6,7] Following in his older brother's footsteps, Oswald joined the Marine Corps at age 17. Qualifying for the Marines requires being able to shoot and hit a target at 100 yards for infantry, with up to 200–500 yards for more advanced placement. Oswald qualified as a sharpshooter. At a distance of 600 feet (265 yards), *twice* the distance between the Kennedy motorcade and Oswald's hideout in the Book Depository building, he averaged a 76% score at slow fire, and 91% at rapid fire.[9,16] Similar to basketball players that can hit 3-point shots in rapid succession while in the rhythm, Oswald excelled at rapid-fire shots on the rifle range. On November 22, Oswald needed only to hit his target at a distance of a mere 59 yards (for the shot that exited Kennedy's throat) and 88 yards (for the fatal head shot)—both easy target ranges for someone with his skills.[9,16] In 1966, another Marine sharpshooter, 25-year-old Charles Whitman, was accurate from an incredible *500 yards* with his Remington Model 700 rifle. He killed 11 people and wounded 31 others from the University of Texas at Austin's clock tower observation deck. Witnesses stated that Whitman had pinpoint accuracy.[17]

Oswald purchased the Mannlicher-Carcano rifle through the mail and used it in his attempt to assassinate U.S. Army General Edwin Walker at his home in April 1963. He created detailed maps, pictures, and sketches portraying his plot to kill Walker, but failed after trying to target him through a window. Seven months later, he discovered that an even bigger target was coming to Dallas—and would be driving directly in front of the Texas Book Depository where he worked.[8]

Oswald believed that fate had put him in Dallas at that moment in history. The target, to this point, hadn't mattered that much—assassinating any important leader could transform him into a great man. He was convinced that he had special talents to offer the world and that he, like Dostoyevsky's Raskolnikov, could morally break laws in service of his own lofty goals.[18]

Oswald moved into *operational space*[7] (by creating a sniper's nest) the day before Kennedy's visit. The motorcade route was published in the newspaper and everyone around Dealey Plaza was excited to discuss it. Oswald would have noted the hairpin turn from Main to Houston and Elm Streets. Kennedy would be a slow-moving, essentially stationary target—very well within his skill range.[8,9] Oswald's research on the motorcade route and his planning, preparation, and implementation were a *pathway* warning behavior.[7]

4. *Novel aggression*: A lone-actor terrorist can efficiently shoot many people under high-stress conditions. Terrorists often participate in acts of *novel aggression* to test their courage and skills. *Novel aggression* is defined as an act of violence that appears unrelated to the intended act of concern and that is committed for the first time—typically in order for the perpetrator to test his own ability to carry out a more meaningful (to him) act of violence.[6,7] Just seven months prior to the assassination, Oswald attempted to assassinate U.S. Army General Edwin Walker. Walker was becoming a popular politician with anti-Castro rhetoric sprinkled throughout his speeches. On March 5, 1963, Walker called upon the country to "liquidate the scourge that has descended upon the island of Cuba."[9(p680)] Oswald, perturbed by this incendiary rhetoric, and seeking fame, was on a pathway to violence. He mail-ordered a Mannlicher-Carcano rifle for $21.45 from Klein's sporting goods in Chicago under a fake name. He took surveillance pictures of the areas around Walker's house.[9,10,12]

On April 10, 1963, Oswald fired a single shot from a fence lattice 40 yards away from the back of the general's home. He barely missed Walker's head as the general was seated at his desk. The bullet was deflected and hit the wall. The next day Oswald was angry that he had missed and bragged about how foolish the police were for getting the bullet and caliber of the rifle wrong, as reported in the news. Walker escaped with only minor cuts to his arm from a few slivers of bullet. The FBI was unaware of Oswald's role in Walker's shooting until after Kennedy's death, when Marina disclosed his involvement.[8,9,10,12]

Oswald's *novel aggression* gave him the courage, resolve, and confidence to shoot at Kennedy's motorcade. This is why predatory violence can be committed in a calm and accurate fashion—the commission of novel aggression (a warning behavior) acts as a sort of dry run or dress rehearsal.[7] It is an important factor in explaining why Oswald did not panic or change his mind at the last second before shooting Kennedy. He was an expert with rifles and his (albeit unsuccessful) attack on Walker had prepared him psychologically for another, bigger target.[11]

5. *Last resort* is evidence of a "violent action imperative" and/or "time imperative"; it may be a signal of desperation or distress. It is often the result of an unexpected triggering event, or one which is anticipated, involving a loss in love and/or work. The subject believes he has no other choice and must act *now*.[7]

Oswald's relationship with his wife Marina was tumultuous. While they were in New Orleans, he tried to compel her to conspire with him to hijack an airplane to Cuba, but she resisted. They fought often. In 1963 Oswald was living in a rooming house in Dallas in order to be close to work, and thus was separated from Marina and their children, whom he visited on weekends. On November 21, just a day before the assassination, another rift had been brewing between the two. Well aware of the choice between killing the president and continuing on with a life he found deeply unsatisfying, Oswald went home to Marina and tried to reconcile with her by giving her a kiss, which she refused twice. On a third attempt, he went so far as to physically block her from leaving the bedroom, demanding a kiss. She was still angry, but kissed him only to comply with his manipulative demand.[8,10,11]

When Marina asked Oswald why he was there that day, he said, "Because I'm tired of living alone and because I get lonesome for my girls."[8] Marina told him that she preferred her friends over him and that she neither loved nor needed him, a devastating rejection. He offered to buy her a washing machine, but she rejected that overture as well.

She said later, "I was smiling inside, but I had a serious expression on my face."[8] Her repeated rejections of Oswald were her way of pushing him to work on their relationship, but when she said that she would never move to Dallas with him, Oswald had the excuse he needed, the freedom to finally act and, as he saw it, to become a major figure on the world stage. If Marina was not going to be with him, then he had no other viable alternative. With the president arriving the next day, Oswald's thinking became increasingly binary, simplistic, and absolute.[14] His decision to assassinate the president, to transform himself into a great hero, had just crystallized. On November 22, 1963, Lee left the gold wedding band he had purchased in Minsk for Marina in a cup on the dresser in his room—a symbol of his triggering event and desperate *last resort warning behavior*.[7,11]

Oswald also exhibited eight positive *distal characteristics* commonly seen in lone-actor targeted violence.

1. *Personal grievance and moral outrage*: Personal grievance is often defined by a major loss in love or work, feelings of anger and humiliation, and the blaming of others. *Moral outrage* is typically a vicarious identification with a group that has suffered or has been victimized, even though the lone-actor terrorist usually has not experienced the suffering himself. Much of Lee Harvey Oswald's life was defined by advocating for Leftist causes, such as the common worker, often seen as exploited by the wealthy and powerful.[6,7] He relished and amplified those beliefs, which grew more resilient and resistant to challenge.
Oswald harbored a grievance against both the American and Soviet systems.[14] Similar to those who participated in the January 6, 2021, U.S. Capitol attack, Oswald held a grudge against governments or symbols of governments that he despised for their perceived wrongs against others. He felt rejected by both American and Soviet governments[14] and held a moral outrage against those systems (see Chapter 9).
2. *Framed by an ideology*: The presence of beliefs that justify the subject's intent to act. This can be a religious belief system, a political philosophy, a secular commitment, a one-issue conflict, or an idiosyncratic justification. Beliefs are usually superficial and are selected to justify violence.[6,7] At age 15, Oswald discovered socialist literature. During his time in the Marines, he had a tendency to blame uncomfortable situations in which he found himself (e.g., marching orders) on "capitalists" in the government. While stationed in Japan in 1957, he was nicknamed "Osvaldovich" by fellow Marines. He believed that a Karl Marx form of government would alleviate the capitalist problem.[8–10]

    Oswald disliked the United States so much that he defected to the Soviet Union, expecting to be received as a person of great importance; he was disappointed when this did not occur. He cut his wrist when the Russian government decided to send him back to America. This manipulative tactic worked, and he was sent to Minsk under surveillance by the KGB. Just as he had disliked other places in his career, Oswald now began to dislike the Soviet system, claiming that it was not a true representation of Marxism but rather a perverted form of Communism. He believed that fate had delivered him a special assignment. When Kennedy came to town, he saw a chance to carry out violent behavior toward somebody much more important than General Walker—the president of the United States. Indeed, while handcuffed, Oswald boldly displayed a clenched fist—a Leftist salute.[8–10,11] Anders Breivik, having just killed numerous young attendees of a multicultural event, stood before the court in Norway with his arm outstretched in a Nazi salute.[19] Breivik, unlike Oswald, had access to digital communication. He would spark a flame in terms of what a lone-actor terrorist can achieve by distributing a manifesto before his attack—framed by an ideology.

3. *Failure to affiliate*: The experience of rejecting or being rejected by a radical, extremist, or other group with which the subject initially wished to affiliate. Retired FBI agent Kathleen Puckett[20] was the first to describe the failure to affiliate in a group of lone-actor terrorists. These men are often viewed by terrorist cells with suspicion or indifference.[7] Oswald's *failure to affiliate* with Russia, Cuba, or any other Communist country was a distal characteristic of a potential violent attack.[11] Just as a member of the Muslim community in the West might try to join the Islamic State in Syria and ultimately fail, rejected individuals may return to the West and commit acts of terror there. Timothy McVeigh, the Oklahoma City bomber, was so extreme in his views that members of right-wing militias rejected him.[21] The intelligence community today closely monitors foreign terror groups as well as individuals that try and fail to affiliate with them.

4. *Thwarting of occupational goals*: A major setback or failure in a planned academic and/or occupational life course. Oswald had a very unstable academic, military, and work history. He attended 11 different schools, was chronically truant, and warranted a mental health evaluation in New York. He was court martialed by the military. He had trouble building a successful career due to his own behavior. Marina insisted that they move to New Orleans after he tried to assassinate General Walker. There, he contrived a doomed plan to hijack a plane to Cuba. He then tried to defect to Russia once more by traveling to the Soviet Union in Mexico City. He eventually moved back to Dallas and was briefly employed at the Texas Book Depository before the assassination.[8–11,14]

5. *Mental illness*: Evidence of a major mental disorder by history or in the present. The subject's extreme ideology helps to reduce anxiety surrounding the mental disorder; alternatively, symptoms may help to advance the attack (for example, suicidal thoughts and depression become motivations for martyrdom; delusions of grandeur solidify commitment).[6,7] An examination of Oswald's psychiatric records yields information about his character, temperament, and unstable occupational and relationship history, as well as the development of his EOBs (as opposed to delusions or obsessions).

Lee Harvey Oswald was born in 1939 in New Orleans. His mother, Marguerite, was widowed when she was seven months pregnant with Lee. Marguerite, with only a ninth-grade education, had two other young boys, John and Robert. Facing serious economic hardship, she placed her boys in an orphanage when Lee was three. Marguerite had an affair with a married man whom she eventually married, but the relationship soon ended in her own divorce, and Lee returned to live with her at age four when she moved to Dallas. Lee attended nearly a half dozen different schools. After a tumultuous series of school absences, a family domestic relations court eventually declared that Lee had been excessively absent from school and that he was "beyond the control of his mother".[2,3,22] He was eventually remanded to a youth home for a mental health evaluation, where psychologist Dr. Irving Sokolow determined that his IQ (WISC) was 118.

The only psychiatrist's report on Oswald known to exist was completed by Renatus Hartogs, MD, PhD, in 1953, when Oswald was only 13.[8-10,14] It was provided to his court-appointed probation officer, and reads, in part:

> This 13-year-old well built boy has superior mental resources and functions only slightly below his capacity level in spite of chronic truancy from school which brought him into Youth House. No finding of neurological impairment or psychotic mental changes could be made. Lee has to be diagnosed as "personality pattern disturbance with schizoid features and passive-aggressive tendencies." Lee has to be seen as an emotionally, quite disturbed youngster who suffers under the impact of really existing emotional isolation and deprivation, lack of affection, absence of family life and rejection by a self-involved and conflicted mother. Although Lee denies that he is in need of any other form of help other than "remedial" one, we gained the definite impression that Lee can be reached through contact with an understanding and very patient psychotherapist and if he could be drawn at the same time into group psychotherapy. We arrive therefore at the recommendation that he should be placed on probation under the condition that he seek help and guidance through contact with a child guidance clinic, where he should be treated preferably by a male psychiatrist who could substitute, to a certain degree at least, for the lack of a father figure. At the same time, his mother should be urged to seek psychotherapeutic guidance through contact with a family agency. If this plan does not work out favorably and Lee cannot cooperate in this treatment plan on an out-patient's basis, removal from the home and placement could be resorted to at a later date, but it is our definite impression that treatment on probation should be tried out before the stricter and therefore possibly more harmful placement approach is applied to the case of this boy. The Big Brother Movement could be undoubtedly of tremendous value in this case and Lee should be urged to join the organized group activities of his community, such as provided by the PAL or YMCA of his neighborhood. Renatus Hartogs, M.D., Ph.D., Senior Psychiatrist. [9(p535)]

As Hartog's report cited outdated diagnostic criteria, a brief review of diagnostic considerations is needed. A schizoid personality disorder is not diagnosable in children, and passive-aggressive personality was dropped from the psychiatric nomenclature long ago. Lee's modern DSM-5 diagnosis at age 13 is subject to debate. For the purposes of our analysis here, Hartog's report was reviewed by neurodevelopmental expert and psychiatrist John Constantino, as well as two other child psychiatrists, Tashalee Brown and Emily Slat, at Washington University in St. Louis. Initially I withheld the subject's identity from all three experts. They were each told that the 1953 report was on someone named "Lee." They noted that Lee kept to himself, and that he had restricted interests and an inflexible, rigid mother (possible genetic component); interestingly, they all believed that Lee might be on the autism spectrum disorder. They expanded their considerations to acknowledge that although an autism diagnosis was reasonable, Lee also showed social anxiety symptoms and might have been diagnosed with reactive attachment disorder.

According to a 1967 psychiatric textbook by Kaplan and Freedman, a schizoid personality is characterized by "a tendency to avoid close or prolonged relationships with other people. A corollary of this is the tendency to think autistically."[25(p941)] The diagnosis of autism spectrum disorder in the context of violence is controversial as it relates to fixations seen in attackers such as Adam Lanza (Sandy Hook school shooter), Alek Minassian (incel), and Jacob Chansley (Qanon Shaman). The form of these young men's beliefs was similar (extreme and overvalued), yet as discussed in other chapters, the content of those beliefs was quite varied, depending on their individual subcultures.

The concept of attachment theory posits that primary caregivers who are available and responsive to a child's needs allow the child to develop a sense of security. Failure to form these secure attachments early in life can have a negative impact on behavior in later childhood and throughout adult life, and may even increase the risk of violence.[21,22] Applying attachment theory here, we see the probable impact of Oswald's devastating losses of primary parental objects. His mother was erratic, needy, and unstable, and had irrational outbursts.[3,9-11,22] He did not know his father, nor was there ever a stable father figure in his life. In seventh grade Lee and his mother lived with Lee's older brother and his wife, Marge; it was not a harmonious household. One day Lee got into an argument with Marge over the television and pulled out a pocket knife.[8-11] As an adolescent, Oswald embraced Marxist ideology and sought to gain the approval and acceptance he was missing from his own parents through overvalued, narcissistic (relished, amplified, and defended) homicidal aggression, which compelled him toward targeted violence, sanctioned by an externally perceived code of moral authority (Karl Marx).[3,11,21]

6. *Changes in thinking and emotion*: Thoughts and their expression become more strident, simplistic, and absolute. Argument ceases and preaching begins. Persuasion yields to imposition of one's beliefs on others. There is no critical analysis of theory or opinion; the mantra "don't think, just believe" is adopted. Emotions typically move from anger and argument to contempt and disdain for others' beliefs, to disgust toward the out-group and a willingness to homicidally aggress against them. Violence is cloaked in self-righteousness and the pretense of superior belief.[6,7] Engagement with others in virtual and/or real-life settings may greatly diminish or cease once the subject has moved into operational space, which means commencement of planning and preparation for the attack. Oswald gradually became more rigid in his political beliefs, as evidenced by the increasingly extreme lengths he went to support them.[8,14] Unstable personality features[3,11] stimulated anger, rejection, anxiety, and moral outrage.
7. *Creativity and innovation*: Evidence of inspired tactical thinking. The planned terrorist act is creative and/or innovative.[6,7] Just a few days before the assassination, Oswald read about Kennedy's motorcade and the plan to pass right in front of his window at work. He developed the somewhat surprising plan to create a sniper's nest in an area that he could easily use to move into operational space. Sniper perches were also creatively utilized by Charles Whitman, the University of Texas clock tower shooter, and Stephen Paddock, the Las Vegas concert shooter. More recently, Robert Crimo III, like Oswald, perched on a rooftop with a rifle, killing seven and wounding 30 others during a Fourth of July parade in Chicago's Highland Park. He posted a video of himself sitting on a bed rapping with a newspaper; a poster featuring Lee Harvey Oswald was hanging on the wall behind him.[23]
8. *Criminal violence*: Evidence of instrumental criminal violence in the subject's past, demonstrating a capacity and a willingness to engage in predation for a variety of reasons, such as a history of armed robberies or planned assaults on others for material gain.[6,7] Oswald had a history of violence toward others; as a teenager he struck his mother, and he was violent toward his wife—abuse that escalated after the couple moved to the United States from Russia.[11] While in the military, Oswald was court martialed for striking an officer. He considered hijacking a plane to Cuba, which would have undoubtedly required violent action. He shot at General Walker in a clear assassination attempt. His pattern of criminal violence, based on this collection of events, is clear.[3,8–10,11,14]

DIAGNOSTIC CONSIDERATIONS

When seen through the lens of EOBs, Oswald's actions can be viewed as rational and goal-directed. Two key elements are needed to make a person-centered diagnostic formulation for individuals with EOBs: (1) culture/subculture and (2) personality organization.[14]

Cultural formulation is a tool that can help mental health practitioners gather information about an individual in order to understand how culture and subculture affect and are affected by mental illness.[2,14] It should be noted that formulating a case requires a description, not a diagnostic code. For example, *seppuku* is a form of ritualistic suicide in Japanese culture primarily used to restore honor (see Chapter 10). In such cases, culture is the predominant explanation for the suicide, rather than a diagnosis of major depression. There could be an endless number of diagnostic codes if they were created for every subculture—necessitating an individual assessment.

Second, a new approach in the DSM-5 called the *alternative model for personality disorders* allows relevant impairments in individual personality *traits* to be diagnosed as a disorder, even if the subject does not meet full criteria for a specific type of personality disorder.[2,14] The five traits representing broad domains of human personality/behavior, used worldwide, can be learned using the mnemonic OCEAN (openness, conscientiousness, extroversion, agreeableness, and neuroticism).[24]

A comprehensive cultural formulation of Oswald necessitates a careful analysis of his life story. For our purposes, *culture* refers to systems of knowledge concepts, rules, and practices that are learned and transmitted across generations. Cultures are open dynamic systems that undergo continuous change over time; in the contemporary world most individuals and groups are exposed to multiple cultures that they use to fashion their own identities and to make sense of experience.[2,14] Terrorism comes in "waves" or epochs depending on the latest political or religious fervor. In some cases, as with Oswald's attachment to deviant themes, enduring patterns of inner experience and behavior create their own subcultures that can deviate markedly from the individual's culture of origin.[14]

It can be reasonably proposed that a major cultural influence on Oswald was his adoption of extreme Marxist ideologies, and that this drove the formation of his EOBs. Oswald relished, amplified, and defended these beliefs, which began to take shape in his teenage years as he began to explore opposition to the execution of Julius and Ethel Rosenberg.[9-11] He then began reading Marx and subscribed to a socialist newsletter. His anti-capitalism and pro-socialist beliefs grew more dominant, refined, and resistant to challenge over time.[11]

Turning back to Oswald's personality organization,[3] as noted, the DSM-5 allows the diagnosis of a personality disorder based on an individual's unique traits—even if they don't meet all of the criteria for a specific personality disorder (narcissistic, borderline, antisocial, etc.)[3,14] This alternative personality model can be used to develop a person-centered process to facilitate a practical diagnostic assessment.[14] Oswald's childhood was chaotic, and his mother was erratic and emotionally unstable—major risk factors for a neurotic personality organization.[3,22] He found comfort in a newly acquired political ideology as an adolescent. He began to develop an over-involvement in deviant types of political activism. He engaged in self-injurious behavior, domestic violence, and grandiose fantasies of becoming a hero.[8-11] Such traits are commonly seen in borderline and narcissistic personality disorders.[21] He had trouble functioning in multiple domains of life: work, love, family, and community. Utilizing DSM-5 diagnostic criteria,[2,14] Lee Harvey Oswald could well be diagnosed with maladaptive personality traits[3] (a neurotic and borderline personality organization) and EOBs in a Marxist subculture. Diagnosis of a higher functioning autism spectrum disorder and problems with attachment may also be considered in light of the report from his examining psychiatrist in his early years. His intelligence level was considered normal or high.

Though potentially disabling and certainly problematic for those around Oswald, none of these diagnoses provides exculpatory evidence that would support an insanity defense, were he to be put on trial today for his crimes. Instead, they are evidence that he did *not* suffer from a psychotic mental disorder, and that he was aware of the wrongfulness of his actions.

THREAT ASSESSMENT: THWARTING THE ATTACK ON JFK

The list of TRAP-18 items here reveal that Lee Harvey Oswald displayed several proximal warning signs and distal characteristics that may be expected to precipitate a violent attack. Having several proximal warning signs at the same time constitutes an even higher risk[7]; as such, analysis indicates that Oswald posed a serious threat as a lone-actor terrorist. His failed attempt to assassinate General Walker was not known to the FBI until after Kennedy's death, but other proximal warning behaviors and distal characteristics were apparent. Based on decades of research and with full access to existing records on Oswald, we now know that his failure to affiliate with the Soviet Union, as well as the many other factors discussed herein, could have been used to better assess the threat he might have posed. The FBI had already been monitoring him,[8] and a modern-day joint-terrorism task force presence may have proved helpful in 1963. We can only speculate on whether Kennedy's Secret Service detail could have been more vigilant regarding Oswald.

Imagine a person who leaves the U.S. military due to his disenchantment with the United States and travels to Russia, where he tries but fails to affiliate with Vladimir Putin's regime. He would be immediately flagged as a security threat upon his return to the United States. Utilizing the same scientific correlates of the TRAP-18, *Oswald would also have been flagged* as a threat after failing to affiliate with a Cold War adversary, the Soviet Union. It is critical to understand that a structured, scientifically validated tool, such as the TRAP-18, allows the highest-quality analysis of symptoms and behavior, in the context of DSM-5 subculture and personality traits, while leaving out other data that do not reliably inform threat assessment (race, religion, dress, outward show, etc.).

In the final analysis, had they existed at the time, TRAP-18 indicators and DSM-5 diagnostic criteria could have been assimilated to prevent the assassination of President John F. Kennedy. The U.S. Secret Service could have ordered Oswald to stay away from work and Dealey Plaza that day. The limousine bubbletop could have been deployed and JFK could still have met with crowds, well away from buildings with open windows. Indeed, the Secret Service has improved its tactical protection, and subsequent attacks on Gerald Ford (twice) and Ronald Reagan (a close call) were unsuccessful. Unfortunately, the TRAP-18[13,14] did not exist in 1963, and few of the warning signs and behavioral characteristics of lone-actor violence had yet been formally identified. It is important to note, however, that any retrospective analysis will also have unavoidable hindsight bias.

TRIAL AND SENTENCING CONSIDERATIONS

Once Oswald was arrested for the murder of Dallas police officer J. D. Tippit, he would have faced a multitude of serious state and federal charges. He would have been charged with the assassination of the president, the attempted assassination of Governor Connally, the murder of Officer Tippet, and the attempted murder of General Walker.[9] His defense attorneys would likely have consulted psychiatrists for forensic opinions regarding any psychiatric diagnoses that could have affected his ability to know the wrongfulness of his actions. Facing the death penalty, his defense team would be challenged by overwhelming pieces of key physical evidence—Oswald's fingerprints on the rifle, the photograph of him holding the rifle, ballistics reports, and numerous interrogation reports, as well as eyewitness reports. The shot trajectories would be easy to prove as having come from one direction and from one rifle—the one stashed at the Texas Book Depository building. At trial, a jury would have found Oswald guilty, probably in a short period of time, and a plea deal would have been unlikely. Although conspiracy theorists like to claim that the mafia, the CIA, or other groups were responsible, in the mid-1960s, before these stories had had time to gain momentum in American society, they would have amounted to nothing more than farfetched defense strategies that no competent attorney would have pursued.[9] Oswald's statements during his interrogations would have been seen as simple lies. He was not a patsy. It was his rifle. He was in the building on the 6th floor. He claimed he was a Marxist. He tried to shoot General Walker. He was using a fake name. The list goes on.

Given that this would have been a death penalty case, the capital defense team (at least in the modern era) would raise mitigating circumstances (such as prior mental illness or psychological traumas) at the time of final sentencing. Indeed, Oswald had a very troubled past, but his normal to above average intelligence and evidence of a carefully planned assassination would likely have resulted in a death penalty verdict.

The fact that Oswald was a former U.S. Marine who traveled to Russia, lived in many different places, and visited a Soviet Union in Mexico City sounds like something straight out of a spy novel. But when seen through the light of the diagnostic considerations here, it is quite evident to me that he would meet today's definition of personality disorder with borderline and narcissistic traits.[8-10,14] As psychologist David Abrahamsen wrote in 1967, denying the crime increased Oswald's narcissistic sense of power and intensified his gratification. He held answers, he likely believed, answers that no one else knew. He projected onto the media what he was feeling inside, "I'm just a patsy." Americans listening in were the patsy.

7

Fame at Any Cost—Sandy Hook

People speak sometimes about the "bestial" cruelty of man, but that is terribly unjust and offensive to beasts, no animal could ever be so cruel as a man, so artfully, so artistically cruel.

—Fyodor Dostoyevsky[1]

Not all mass killers are motivated by one-sided political ideas or racism. Some, feeling lost in obscurity, seek fame, at the cost of their futures or even their lives. Mark David Chapman couldn't *be* John Lennon, but the next best thing was to be forever connected to the ex-Beatle as his murderer. There have been many others with the same kind of grandiose and relished thinking. In fact, half of the 10 most widely covered mass shootings in the United States since 1999 were perpetrated by individuals classified as "fame-seekers," as characterized by their actions both before and after the incidents, according to a study published in the journal *Aggression and Violent Behavior*.[2] Authors Jason Silva and Emily Greene-Colozzi identified 45 cases out of 308 incidents of mass shootings between 1996 and 2018 that they categorized as having been committed by "fame-seeking" perpetrators. "Fame-seeking mass shooters are differentiated from other mass shooters by their explicit desire for infamy,"[2(p25)] they wrote, noting that the media is quick to take the bait. Thus, mass killing for the purpose of fame-seeking can be seen as is its own separate type of subculture. It has a characteristic pattern of behavior which embraces the culture with a passionate set of emotions—something on which researchers are now homing in.

A SUBCULTURE OF MASS MURDER

In December 2012, Adam Lanza's mother Nancy had just finished decorating her home for Christmas. Garlands twisted around two white pillars at the home's entrance. Inside, the house was furnished with pristine white leather furniture and seasonal greenery. It hardly seemed like a breeding ground for hatred. Nonetheless, 11 days before Christmas, Lanza shot his mother in the head four times.[3]

After killing his mother, Lanza drove to his old school, Sandy Hook Elementary. Armed with his mother's Bushmaster XM15-E2S rifle and 10 magazines with 30 rounds each, Lanza entered the school and yelled, "Put your hands up," as he began shooting. When Lanza was done, 20 children and 6 adults were dead. He took his own life as the police closed in on the scene.[3,4]

Parents hugged their children a little tighter that night. President Barack Obama shed tears on national television.[5] The tragedy was on such a scale that the Lanza home, a reminder of that day, was eventually demolished and the school building itself would later be replaced by a new one. But the emotional damage could never be undone, and the trauma of the community, rekindled over and over again in the years since by overvalued conspiracy theories (such as the falsehood that the shooting was staged by anti-gun advocates), lives on.[6] The ensuing investigation revealed that Lanza expressed a "scorn for humanity," an interest in pedophilia, a contempt for overweight people, and a long list of grievances.[3,7]

LANZA'S MENTAL HEALTH HISTORY

Voluminous files, photos, medical records, and videos were released by the state of Connecticut in the wake of the shooting.[3] Among other revelations, they portrayed how Nancy Lanza struggled to help her son Adam, who was diagnosed with autism spectrum disorder at a young age. He had sensory issues, language delays, anxiety, and repetitive behaviors. She and her husband took him to see psychiatrists, including experts at Yale University, who recommended special education and rigorous social therapeutic supports to help him.[3]

Lanza was fixated on topics in which many other children might also be interested. He liked to keep his socks even and had some sensory integration issues (tags had to be removed from his clothing). He was a creative child who loved to play video games and write stories—though his stories were often dark. One was called "The Big Book of Granny" in which an old woman with a gun in a crane killed others. He also wrote a story called "Dora the Berserker" (perhaps a darker fantasy and response to the popular cartoon, *Dora the Explorer*), in which a character likes hurting others, especially children.[3]

Yale psychiatrist Robert King described Lanza at age 14 as "pale, gaunt, awkward ... and standing rigidly with his eyes downcast and declining to shake hands, tremulous with discomfort and looking miserable."[8(np)] Nancy told Dr. King that her son "was much more relaxed at home, and his stiffness and tension was [sic] due to being here." Dr. King described other elements of the interview. "What is a friend?" King asked Lanza. "It is difficult to define—in whose culture do you refer?" Lanza intellectually answered. If he was given wishes, what would he wish for? Lanza replied, "I would wish that whatever was granting the wishes would not exist."[8(np)]

King prescribed Lanza an antidepressant after diagnosing him with autism spectrum disorder and noting that he suffered from obsessions, including the fear of contamination from touching metal objects like doorknobs, as well as from the affectionate touch of his mother. The medication made Lanza dizzy and sweat profusely, and it affected his thinking. After just three days he stopped taking it.[3,7-10]

Over the course of his school years, Lanza was described as a quiet, shy boy who never made trouble and had friends; he was described as friendly to others. His sixth-grade teacher stated he was "a normal child with no oddities and there were no reports of bullying or teasing." In intermediate school he was "respectful and cooperated with others." In high school, teachers noted that he "did not have good social skills," was "withdrawn," and "a quiet person." The concluding paragraph of the "Education and Mental Health" section of the Connecticut investigation report stated: "It is unknown what contribution, if any, the shooter's mental health issues made to his attack. . . . Those mental health professionals who saw him did not see anything that would have predicted his future behavior."[3(np)]

In retrospect, some have speculated that Adam Lanza might have had schizophrenia,[4] but I conclude that there is weak evidence that he had delusions or hallucinations, disorganized speech or behavior, or other overt signs of the illness. Instead, it appears that he idolized mass shooters, including Columbine shooters Eric Harris and Dylan Klebold. Some speculated that he was a pedophile and saw himself as "saving children" from adults.[9,10] Nevertheless, psychiatrists were ill-equipped to properly detect whatever was growing within him.

THIN PEOPLE ARE GRACEFUL

Although Lanza held obsessions and tried to maintain extreme cleanliness, he also nurtured passionately held beliefs often seen in overvalued ideas. At first they centered on his desire to be thin. He developed signs of anorexia, writing that "[o]nly thin people are graceful." Amid a culture that prizes thinness, Lanza apparently despised fat people, and copied a list he found online of 35 reasons to "hate food and fat people." This included intense beliefs such as, "Food is mean and sneaky. It tricks you into eating it and it works on you from the inside out making you fat, bloated, ugly and unhappy."[10(np)] While most people do not develop such extreme body image distortions, the list Lanza copied espouses beliefs commonly shared by those with eating disorders—a desire to be thin at any cost.

Lanza shared his perverse ideology regarding food with others he interacted with in online forums. At the time of his death, he was 6 feet tall and weighed only 112 pounds; this yields a body mass index of 15.2, which meets the weight loss requirement for a diagnosis of anorexia nervosa.[3] The anorexic's fear of being overweight is held with an extraordinary degree of conviction, and it does not yield when faced with evidence of how harmful this behavior can be. Although the belief is preoccupying and the individual acts on it unquestioningly, leading to sustained patterns of abnormal eating behavior, it is not considered to be delusional; instead, it is considered by many to be an overvalued idea.[11,12] Of note, some investigators believe that starvation might result in worsening cognitive problems, while others have disagreed.[13,14]

While his weight was something that others could outwardly see as a problem, Lanza also had an extreme fixation on joining the ranks of history's worst mass murderers. After his death a spreadsheet of some 400 such individuals was found on his computer, including meticulously detailed accounts of their crimes.[3,10] Such a list would have taken a great deal of time to compose. Lanza ranked these offenders according to the number of victims killed or wounded, and listed their genders and causes of death. It is not difficult to envision Lanza relishing in the compilation of the spreadsheet, as well as in the idea of the fame that resulted from these killings.

I propose that this is where Lanza developed his *internet cognitive isoform*. As discussed later in Chapter 9, this is a process by which the brain uses cognitive shortcuts to make inferences about the world—which often turn out to be incorrect. The brain takes ambiguous or complex information and interprets it in the simplest possible terms.[15] In Lanza's online world, the most notorious mass murderers seemed to have achieved something positive, something he fantasized for himself: a way out of his own life, and with the additional benefit of fame. Lanza posted nearly 300 times in an online forum called "Shocked Beyond Belief,"[16,17] where he used the username "Smiggles."[8,14,16] In one post Lanza wrote, "The best movie I've seen about a mass shooting was from *Lifetime*. Other than the issue of portraying Richard Farley [Sunnyvale, California mass shooter] as a cute engineer instead of a creepy technician, its immense amount of accurate details warrants its 'based on a true story' status."[16(p9)]

In another post Lanza relishes a video he found online about Cleveland Elementary School shooter Patrick Purdy, who shot and killed 5 schoolchildren and wounded 32, as well as other mass killers. Lanza wrote, "I just came across this one which includes a ton of footage I've never seen elsewhere. It even shows some of Patrick Purdy's fabled army men! Mass murderers included in it: Colin Ferguson, Charles Whitman, James Huberty, Julio Gonzalez, George Hennard, Patrick Purdy, Thomas Hamilton."[16(p10)]

After Anders Breivik's murder of 77 people in Norway, Lanza wrote that "finally" someone had topped Woo bum-kon, who killed 56 people in South Korea in 1982. Lanza also noted that when a mass shooter's motives are a "mystery," the case gets more attention.[9,16]

In an exchange with a fellow online gamer, Lanza stated, "I incessantly have nothing other than scorn for humanity."[7,(np)] At some level, Lanza must have realized that the killing of small children had a special element of depravity that would ensure big headlines. Misanthropic sentiments have also been espoused by other shooters, such as Elliot Rodger (who killed 6 and injured 14), as well as by Ted Kaczynski (the Unabomber). This scorn for others formed the basis of their extreme overvalued beliefs (EOBs). Lanza's thinking became more refined over time, his warped moral stance increasingly binary, simplistic, and absolute, culminating in a plan to murder children, while intentionally leaving his motivation a mystery in order to garner even more attention.

Some of the shooters idolized by Lanza had moral and lofty reasons for their homicidal acts—a subculture born in 1999 with the Columbine High School massacre. Shooters Dylan Klebold and Eric Harris saw themselves as saviors, of a sort, of fellow classmates who were bullied and mistreated at school. Psychologist and mass shooter expert Dr. Peter Langman has compiled transcripts on many shootings, including Columbine[17-19]. In a classroom film project created by Klebold and Harris, called *Hitmen for Hire*, the two are seen dancing, cursing, and relishing the act of shooting and killing students at Columbine High School. In one scene, a student being bullied by others wants to hire them to protect him:

STUDENT: I'll pay anything!
ERIC HARRIS: All right. It's 20 dollars a day in school. You know we can't have any weapons on school grounds.
STUDENT: That's fine—I'll get them off the property!
ERIC HARRIS: All right. We'll protect you in school. Take away any bullies that are picking on you. And off school grounds we could relocate this person. That would be a thousand dollars.
STUDENT: Thank you so much![18]

Lanza was also particularly fixated on James Holmes (the Aurora, Colorado, movie theater shooter), and Jared Loughner (the Tucson, Arizona, mass shooter). He was enthralled by media reports and eager to learn from them. Three days before the Sandy Hook shooting, Lanza sent an email to a cyber-friend, referring to James Holmes as "Holmie" (a reference to the slang term *homie*, meaning friend)[9]:

As far as the Holmies go . . . well, the .gif of him dancing on a llama was cute. I guess that's all I can say about the whole Holmie thing since I can't really relate to it. I don't understand why there weren't the "he's just a poor misunderstood puppy who needs help" type flocking around Jared Loughner since that spiel ostensibly applied to him more than James Holmes. And speaking more generally, I don't really understand why Aurora shooting was considered such a big deal all-around, as if such a thing had never happened before. It's not like 1984.[9(p121)]

In her article "Mass Media Reporting and Enabling of Mass Shootings" Jennifer Murray explains that Lanza appears to be depicting both Loughner and Holmes as weak and inferior killers. He admires the Virginia Tech and Columbine shooters, but admonishes more recent ones just three days before carrying out his own massacre. Five months prior to the Sandy Hook massacre, Adam Lanza, manifesting a "last resort" behavior, wrote to another cyber-friend, "My interest in mass murdered [sic] has been perfunctory for such a long time. The enthusiasm I had back when Virginia Tech happened feels like it's been gone for a hundred billion years. I don't care about anything. I'm just done with it all."[9(p121)]

These writings are evidence of Lanza's intense planning and fantasizing prior to his massacre. In current psychiatry clinical guides, such fantasies are not routinely considered by psychiatrists. Murray goes on to explain that shooters like Lanza revel in the "media thirst and cycle of coverage" of prior shooters, and that they have an adrenaline-charged luscious fantasy reminiscent of serial killers.[8]

LANZA'S HYPOTHETICAL TRIAL

Had Adam Lanza survived his attack, he would have faced overwhelming evidence of his heinous crimes, with multiple counts of homicide with cruel and depraved actions as aggravating factors. The death penalty was repealed by the Connecticut legislature in 2012, so prosecutors would have been unable to pursue that option.[20] Lanza would have been subject to several court-ordered and private psychiatric evaluations. After being found competent to stand trial, his attorneys would almost certainly have encouraged him to plead the insanity defense. Similar to the role of the autism spectrum diagnosis in the case of Alex Minassian[21] (who used a rental van to kill 10 in Toronto, Canada), Lanza's diagnosis may have provided a rationale for the defense to argue that he was insane. However, his relatively high or normal intellectual functioning would have made it difficult to establish a diagnosis of severe mental disorder (impaired IQ plus other disorders can often be useful to establish a severe mental disorder in insanity cases).

The diagnosis of a psychotic mental illness, or schizophrenia spectrum disorder (e.g., delusional disorder) might also have been made.[4] Experts could have argued that Lanza experienced many delusions and obsessions (from his compulsive cleanliness to his eating disorder and fixation on mass shootings). The defense experts might have opined that Lanza's mental disease or defect due to "schizophrenia"[4] or "delusional disorder" prevented him from appreciating the criminality of his behavior, and/or from conforming that behavior to the requirements of the law. In contrast, prosecutors, presenting strong evidence of Lanza's intent, could have introduced evidence from his computer hard drive, which included Lanza's meticulously crafted spreadsheet of prior mass murders and his membership in a depraved digital subculture. While this evidence might have been used in an attempt to establish that Lanza didn't know right from wrong, it would not have been effective. Analogously, members of the Proud Boys who participated in the January 6, 2021, uprising could not have been found insane in criminal proceedings, because although they could argue that they were misled by their subculture, they nevertheless had no mental disorder.[22]

Since the burden of proof for insanity in Connecticut rests with the defense, prosecution experts could have faced a difficult challenge in refuting presumptive evidence of Lanza's "delusions" put forth by his defense team. Instead, by utilizing and distinguishing between the definitions of obsession, delusion, and EOBs, a more concise conclusion could have been reached.[20] One might offer the following opinion: Mr. Lanza held EOBs, not delusions or obsessions, regarding mass shootings. While he clearly had autism spectrum disorder and obsessional thoughts about germs and contamination, he avoided discussing those topics online. Instead, he meticulously studied and relished his identification with prior mass shooters. In that subculture, Lanza methodically cataloged death tolls (which he eagerly ranked) and weapons of choice. Lanza fantasized about this subculture and shared his ideology with others online. The misanthropic beliefs articulated in his internet posts are clear, including his "scorn for humanity"[7] and praise for prior attackers for "accomplishing" higher body counts. While most people consider homicide to be unjustifiable except in instances such as self-defense, Lanza shared the glorification of killing with others. He knew that, above all, killing children would make him special within his subculture and in history. His beliefs grew more dominant, refined, and resistant to challenge over time. He maintained an intense emotional commitment to carrying out violence against his mother and the children of Sandy Hook Elementary School.

As we will discuss in the next chapter, an online subculture likely helped provoke an eerily similar attack at Robb Elementary School in Uvalde, Texas, in 2022.

8
Digital Subcultures

An individual in a crowd is a grain of sand amid other grains of sand, which the wind stirs up at will.
—GUSTAVE LE BON, in *The Crowd, a Study of the Popular Mind (1895)*[1]

Le Bon could never have imagined how his allegory of grains of sand[1] would one day become silicon based. The internet, smart phones, virtual reality, and the technology behind them all have transformed the world in ways that would have been unimaginable to prior generations. Everyone, it seems, is connected, accessing a continual stream of positive reinforcement (likes and positive emojis), engaging in common interests among subcultural groups of unlimited number. But online activity is not always centered around last night's dinner, sports, family photos, or showing off one's latest vacation. A digital subculture of dissatisfaction, racism, and the glorification of violent behavior not only exists, but thrives—producing a well-known *contagion* or "copycat" effect in terrorism.[2] Further complicating matters, according to Sherry Turkle, author of *Alone Together*, virtual life may trump real life for many, especially people who may "feel more comfortable in an unreal place than a real one."[3(p212)] Psychiatrists refer to fixated beliefs as being *pathoplastic* because they mold around a person's subculture.

Recent acts of violence share common themes. The suspects responsible for the 2015 slaughter of nine at a Bible study group in Charleston, South Carolina; the murder of 23 people at a Wal-Mart in El Paso, Texas, in 2019; the mass shooting in Buffalo, New York, in May 2022; and the attack on a crowd in Highland Park, Illinois, in July 2022 were all radicalized online, leaving behind a trail of digital activity.[4–6]

As discussed earlier, *culture* refers to systems of knowledge, concepts, rules, and practices that are learned and include language, religion and spirituality, family structures, life-cycle stages, ceremonial rituals, and moral and legal customs. Many such systems are now transmitted and learned online. As I have used the term *subculture* extensively throughout this discussion, the concept of culture and subculture are important to tease apart. For example, two people who oppose abortion rights might differ considerably from a subcultural standpoint if only one of them believes that killing an abortion-performing doctor is a morally justified act—and yet they share a cultural connection through their opposition to abortion. Religious, political, and other "morally driven" movements can become extreme fixations for those vulnerable to extreme overvalued beliefs (EOBs). Al-Qaeda and White supremacist groups, for example, constitute subcultures that vary significantly from more moderate mainstream cultures that share similar (but less extreme) beliefs.[7] As we shall see, in assessing a threat and attempting to prevent violence, it is critical to consider together an individual's life story, personality traits, and involvement in online subcultures, which can culminate in violence.[7,8]

THE BUFFALO ATTACK

The actions of Payton Gendron, an 18-year-old who committed one of the deadliest massacres in recent American history, serve as a powerful illustration of binary, simplistic, and absolute thinking, with group support, initiated and sustained through his involvement in an online subculture.

On the afternoon of Saturday, May 14, 2022, Gendron killed 10 people and wounded 3 with a legally purchased but modified Bushmaster XM-15 semi-automatic rifle at a Tops Friendly Markets in Buffalo, New York. He wore military gear and a helmet with a GoPro Hero 7 camera attached. Of those shot, 11 were Black and 2 were White; the 10 who lost their lives were Black. Once the police arrived, Gendron put the rifle to his own neck, but the officers talked him into dropping his gun before arresting him.[2,5]

Gendron was part of an online subculture that used the popular online messaging platform Discord. Discord is host to more than 140 million users, and rebranded itself in 2020 with the simple tagline, "Your Place to Talk." Prior to that time, the application was geared toward helping gamers communicate during play. It was, and still is, well-suited for people like Gendron seeking a private or public audience. In a 180-page manifesto published on the server, Gendron discussed the Christchurch, New Zealand, mosques shooter, replacement theory, and his rationale for choosing the Tops Friendly Markets. Replacement theory is the idea that Black and other minoritized groups are actively engaged in an effort to "replace" White people, thereby eliminating the White race. A broad subculture supporting it exists online, and replacement theory has been identified as having inspired other racially motivated attacks.[2,5,6]

Amarnath Amarasingam and Marc-André Argentino, both fellows at the International Centre for the Study of Radicalization, analyzed Gendron's path to violence in depth,[4] finding that while Gendron's written material was extensive, the majority of it was reproduced verbatim from Brenton Tarrant's 2019 manifesto. Tarrant killed 51 and injured 40 at two Christchurch mosques in 2019, and his manifesto has become something of a gold standard to young radicalized

White men, excerpted extensively by subsequent killers. A targeted violent manifesto is defined as "[a] written or spoken communication intended to justify an act of violence against a specific target by articulating self-identified grievances, homicidal intentions, and/or extreme ideologies for committing an attack. Generally composed by a single author before the incident occurs, it sometimes expresses incendiary beliefs and ideas to promote a violent subculture with political, religious, or social themes."[2,(p9)]

The rest of Gendron's manifesto is a detailed instruction manual for others who want to follow in his footsteps, detailing everything right down to the best socks to wear during a mass shooting. Unlike those of previous attackers, however, the manifesto is also accompanied by a 673-page Discord diary or chat log, upon which Gendron posted several times a day between November 18, 2021, and May 12, 2022, two days before the attack.[2,5,6] Gendron instructed those in his Discord network to make his writings public after the attack.

Gendron's manifesto was posted to Google Docs two days before the attack, then subsequently to 8Chan (now called 8kun) and 4Chan, anonymous, anything-goes online forums. These venues are notorious for hosting everything from neo-Nazi content to child pornography, and Gendron later contended that his racist views were the result of the influence of 4Chan postings. He used a camera on his helmet to livestream to the video platform Twitch for about 30 minutes, including his drive to the store and the first two minutes of the attack. Live streaming has become a creative part of mass shooter subculture.[2,5,6]

Several elements came together to trigger Gendron's violence: his growing isolation from friends and family, the impact of 4Chan and "Chan" subculture, the influence of Brenton Tarrant and the Christchurch massacre, and Gendron's growing sense that he "can't even turn back" (*last resort*) from his exhilarating attack plans.[5,6] Gendron also noted that he had "probably spent actual years of my life just being online."[5(p2)]

This is an example of *dependence on the virtual community*, a distal characteristic of the TRAP-18.[8] He was heavily involved in gaming and gaming communities over the years and noted that "the problem with video games is that it leaves you with a false sensation of progress. In reality, you haven't changed anything in the real world. Plus, it can be addictive when it is your only escape."[5(p2)]

At school Gendron had developed some personal grievances. He noted that he was never close with his classmates, and that he had had some "bad experiences with Black people," such as getting in trouble for using a racial slur in reference to a Black student in sixth grade, and being harassed by another student. Gendron became convinced by the "facts" he encountered on 4Chan, and he incorporated into his manifesto and Discord logs a barrage of screenshots relating to Holocaust denial, purported Jewish control of the world, the contribution of White people to America's economy and culture, the supposed contribution of Black people to the crime rate, IQ differences, and the need for racial segregation. These beliefs formed his psychological schema. He further argued that there are genetic differences between Black and White people, and that Black people were having more children than White people because they were receiving government financial support.[5,6]

When these beliefs are viewed in isolation, they might appear on the surface to be delusional. However, when closely examined through the lens of Gendron's digital subculture, it is quite apparent that his moral and other customs are actually a blend of various EOBs.[6]

CHARLESTON ATTACK

The production of a manifesto prior to a terrorist assault is an increasingly ritualized aspect of extreme-right terrorism. The growing number of such manifestos since 2019, along with other digital fragments to justify attacks, has created a body of "literature" upon which extreme-right assailants can draw for intellectual and practical instruction.[2,9]

As noted, Payton Gendron simply copied large portions of Brenton Tarrant's manifesto. But there were others, including one written by Dylann Roof, the 21-year-old who gunned down nine people at a Bible study at the Emanuel African Methodist Episcopal Church in Charleston, South Carolina, in 2015.[2,5] Roof's manifesto was "not bad," Gendron noted, but its impact was limited because he didn't broadcast it live. With his own forthcoming attack in mind, Gendron stated, "livestreaming this attack makes a 1000x greater impact."[5(p5)]

The nine people Roof killed were all Black and included the senior pastor and state senator Clementa C. Pinckney. Another was injured. Roof was apprehended after an extended manhunt and later confessed that he perpetrated the shooting in hopes of igniting a race war.[5]

Roof created his own net venue, a website called "The Last Rhodesian," to spotlight himself posing with symbols of White supremacy and neo-Nazism, as well as his manifesto, in which he outlined his views toward Black people, among other groups. Other photos show Roof wearing camouflage pants and combat boots, posing among the gravestones in a Confederate cemetery, burning an American flag, holding a Confederate flag, and posing shirtless in a bedroom with a handgun pointed at the camera. In another photo, Roof scowls at the camera from a beach on which he's written symbols that are ubiquitous within the White supremacist movement. Roof did not appear to belong to any in-person White supremacist groups and was instead indoctrinated on the internet.[9-13]

Roof was sentenced to death for his actions. As he sits in prison launching appeals, White supremacists are actively promoting him as a hero online.[12]

TARGETING LATINOS

Extreme-right political doctrine, reinforced online, played a dominant role in the deadliest attack aimed at Latinos in modern history. On August 3, 2019, 21-year-old Patrick Wood Crusius killed 23 people and injured 23 others before being arrested. Once again, the message board 8Chan played a role prior to the attack, according to police, as Crusius posted his own manifesto there just 19 minutes before the first 911 call was received.[2,13–15]

In *The Inconvenient Truth*, Crusius wrote, "In general, I support the Christchurch shooter and his manifesto. This attack is a response to the Hispanic invasion of Texas. They are the instigators, not me. I am simply defending my country from cultural and ethnic replacement brought on by an invasion."[14,(p14)]

Referring to his political rationale for his actions, choices of weapons, and personal thoughts, Crusius added:

> My whole life I have been preparing for a future that currently doesn't exist. The job of my dreams will likely be automated. Hispanics will take control of the local and state government of my beloved Texas, changing policy to better suit their needs. They will turn Texas into an instrument of a political coup which will hasten the destruction of our country. The environment is getting worse by the year.[14,(p14)]

He also added that his opinions predated the presidency of Donald Trump, who should not be blamed for the attack in any way.

On February 6, 2020, Crusius was charged with 22 counts of committing a hate crime resulting in death, 22 counts of use of a firearm to commit murder, 23 counts of a hate crime involving an attempt to kill, and 23 counts of use of a firearm during a crime.[16]

In July 2020, the federal court granted a defense motion for more time to investigate "a number of 'red-flag' mitigation themes" as federal prosecutors deliberated on whether to seek a death sentence. In the motion, the defense claimed that Crusius had "severe" lifelong neurological and mental disabilities (he was in special education); that he was treated with antipsychotic medications after his arrest; and that he was in a "psychotic state" when arrested; but they did not raise the insanity defense.[15] Crusius admitted to selecting El Paso as his target to dissuade immigrants from coming to the United States. He was not charged with domestic terrorism because there is currently no applicable federal statute with which to charge individuals who terrorize others. He was sentenced to 90 consecutive life sentences in prison.[16]

MISSED WARNING SIGNS

Before killing 17 people and injuring 17 others on February 14, 2018, at Marjory Stoneman Douglas High School in Parkland, Florida, 19-year-old Nikolas Cruz researched countless mass shootings and weapons and read about homicidal urges. He first started thinking about mass shootings at the age of 13 or 14. Just five months before he carried out the attack, he posted on YouTube, "I am going to be a professional school shooter."[17(p95)] This clear proximal warning behavior of *leakage* and *identification*[7] was missed by law enforcement, in part due to agencies being ill-equipped to handle such a threat. During his trial, the jury was shown 200 online comments and search histories proving that Cruz repeatedly sought information and videos of other mass shootings, such as Columbine, Charlottesville, Aurora, and Las Vegas. The insanity defense was not pursued by his defense attorneys. Instead, Cruz pleaded guilty and was spared the death penalty in 2022 after his defense attorneys presented evidence suggesting he had fetal alcohol syndrome, his mother having used alcohol and cocaine throughout her pregnancy.[18,19]

UVALDE DIGITAL TRAIL

In a deviation from the racist dogma endorsed by the above shooters, the Uvalde, Texas, shooter Salvador Ramos used social media to express rage and misogyny through shocking words and images. Ramos killed 19 children and 2 adults at Robb Elementary School. The *Washington Post* reviewed videos, posts, and text messages sent by 18-year-old Ramos and spoke with four young people who'd talked with him online.[20]

The girls who spoke with the *Post* lived all over the world but met Ramos on Yubo, an app that mixes live-streaming and social networking, and is considered a "Tinder for teens." On Yubo, people can gather in big real-time chatrooms, known as panels, to talk, type messages, and share videos—the digital equivalent of a real-world hangout. Ramos, they said, struck up side conversations with them and followed them onto other platforms, including Instagram, where he could send direct messages whenever he wanted.[20,21]

But over time they saw a darker side, as he posted images of dead cats, texted them strange messages, and joked about sexual assault, they said. In a video from a live Yubo chatroom that listeners had recorded and that was reviewed by the *Post*, Ramos could be heard saying, "Everyone in this world deserves to get raped."[20(p2)]

A 16-year-old boy in Austin who said he saw Ramos frequently in Yubo panels told the *Post* that Ramos made aggressive, sexual comments to young women on the app and sent him a death threat during one panel in January 2020.[21]

"I witnessed him harass girls and threaten them with sexual assault, like rape and kidnapping," said the teen. "It was not like a single occurrence. It was frequent."[21(np)] He and his friends reported Ramos's account to Yubo for bullying and other infractions dozens of times. He never heard back, he said, and the account remained active.[21]

In messages on Facebook, Ramos had also written, "I'm going to shoot my grandmother" and "I'm going to shoot an elementary school" shortly before the attack—a clear *leakage* warning behavior.[20,21]

Ramos was not alone in his unbridled hate, particularly of women. The online forums he used are frequented by many users with the same subcultural contempt for society in general, and for women specifically, and who routinely and openly voice threats of rape and violence.[1,20]

FANTASY AND IDENTIFICATION

The internet and other digital forms of media are powerful tools that enable the development of shared subcultures[7] on a broad range of subjects, many of them productive and positive. One can learn about gardening, sports, vintage movies, or music and become part of a group that relishes a myriad of such topics; people may even adopt the subculture as part of their own identities and fantasize about it, even when offline—and it usually ends there. Unto itself, technology cannot be blamed for the actions of those who use it, any more than a gun can be blamed for the actions of its shooter. But it can give a voice, and support, to nefarious forces and views—relished, amplified, and defended by some. Still, the question remains: Why does one subcultural fixation produce healthy fantasies, while another produces violence? As we shall see in the next chapter, one difference may be the presence of a moral grievance.

9

Morally Reasoned Attacks

Arriving at a belief that is extreme and overvalued is a process. It involves a number of factors, including how the brain works, how we think and reason, and the logic that flows from previously held assumptions. In cases of targeted attacks, the process often stems from a morally reasoned fantasy of cleansing the ambient environment. For this discussion, we move into the domains of biographical narrative and subcultures that shape psychological schemas.

As discussed in Chapter 8, messaging on social media platforms is simple, binary, and simplistic—it is often "for or against" a cause, person, or issue. False messaging can change the outcome of an election and the decision to get vaccinated; it can even influence a decision to commit suicide or homicide. During the 2016 U.S. presidential election, Russia unleashed thousands of fake accounts on Twitter and Facebook with the purpose of influencing the vote in such a way as to help Donald Trump get elected; it also created a web site called "DC Leaks" to display stolen emails from the Democratic National Committee. The site was linked to a Russian hacking entity called Gucifer 2.0.[1] The Russians created fake American personas like "Melvin Redick" and "Alice Donovan" to conduct reconnaissance, hosting, placement, propagation, and saturation. In his photo online, Redick wore a baseball cap backwards and was posed next to his young daughter. He posted a link to DCLeaks.com, and wrote that users should check out "the hidden truth about Hillary Clinton, George Soros and other leaders of the US." The Russians even hijacked mainstream accounts, including @realDonaldTrump, for their simple yet effective operation. U.S. intelligence officials believe that it is highly likely to have influenced the outcome of the election.[2] Terrorists (including ISIS, White supremacist groups, and Al-Qaeda) have also used such tactics to radicalize individuals online.[3] Similarly, the U.S. Capitol attack was fomented by binary, simplistic, and absolute messaging (e.g. "Biden is a communist. Trump won the election. Hang Mike Pence"). The logic of this targeted attack flows in the manner shown here:

> Assumptions about the election being stolen (schema) → anger, contempt, disgust → extreme overvalued belief → cleansing of U.S. Capitol (violence).

This type of transformation occurs over time and requires further exploration.

INTERNET COGNITIVE ISOFORMS

In 2021 FBI agents discovered in Mexico the bodies of two small children that had been reported missing. In a bizarre criminal complaint, a 40-year-old man was indicted for killing his own 2-year-old son and 10-month-old daughter. The FBI alleges that Matthew Coleman was "enlightened" by QAnon and Illuminati conspiracy theories and was receiving visions and signs revealing that his wife possessed serpent DNA and had passed it on to his children. Coleman created a shrine for his children, then later used a spearfishing gun to kill them after surreptitiously taking them to Mexico from their southern California home. He was recently ordered to undergo a mental competency exam.[4,5] The source of his beliefs (delusions or EOBs) has yet to be determined.

In a separate case, Jacob Anthony Chansley (aka Jacob Angeli), known as the Qanon Shaman, participated in COVID-19 lockdown protests and later the U.S. Capitol attack on January 6, 2021. He espoused several extreme overvalued beliefs (EOBs) on social media. These included online subcultural convictions that global elites were running the world, as well as secret rings of pedophiles and satanic worship. He also believed that watching television and listening to the radio actually affect brain waves.[6] Psychological records later revealed that Chansley was diagnosed with a personality disorder while in the military, but was declared fit for duty. He served 27 months in federal prison, was released and now plans to run for Congress.[7] The concept of *cognitive isoforms*, discussed later in this chapter, further reveals how an individual might acquire online an EOB.

GESTALT PSYCHOLOGY

Why does a flipbook trick us into seeing cartoon stick figures that appear to move? In 1912 Max Wertheimer introduced the term *phi phenomenon* (perception of apparent movement). He described the optical illusion of apparent movements when two optical stimuli are presented with alternating high frequency.[8] This explains how cartoons trick the mind—sequential drawings in animation cells are displayed in rapid sequence, giving them life. In times past, discs placed in a circular arrangement and hidden in rapid sequence created the illusion of a spinning wheel, just as modern computers do when their software is taking its time to load, much to the chagrin of their users. In Germany, this observation launched the Gestalt psychology movement—Gestalt meaning "pattern" or "configuration." It explained how humans perceive objects.[9]

A group of laws or principles of Gestalt psychology were introduced in 1923. These laws included: proximity, similarity, closure, symmetry, and common fate. Among other notions, these laws posited that objects are perceptually grouped together by the brain to form patterns that are regular, simple, and orderly (and sometimes misleading). For example, the laws describe how patterns in "connect the dots" images are perceived as figures.[10] The famous image known as

Rubin's vase looks like either two faces or one vase (Figure 9.1). If you see a vase first, it takes time to unlearn this so that you can see the faces.[11] The first image becomes stuck, like an anchor. This is an important factor to keep in mind when we discuss cognitive isoforms and why beliefs are so difficult to unlearn (called *anchoring bias*).[12] This ability to rewire is sometimes referred to as the brain's "plasticity."[13]

Gestalt theory suggests that the mind understands external stimuli as a whole rather than as the sum of parts—the brain fills in the missing gaps. This concept is called *isomorphism*, and it also features in cognitive psychology, where insightful thinking about situations and environmental experiences interact. Gestalt theory has been explicitly applied in anthropology, art, economics, education, industry, mathematics, music, physics, and sociology. When applied to cognition, the theory helps us explain how beliefs form a cognitive pattern that can lean toward EOBs.[14]

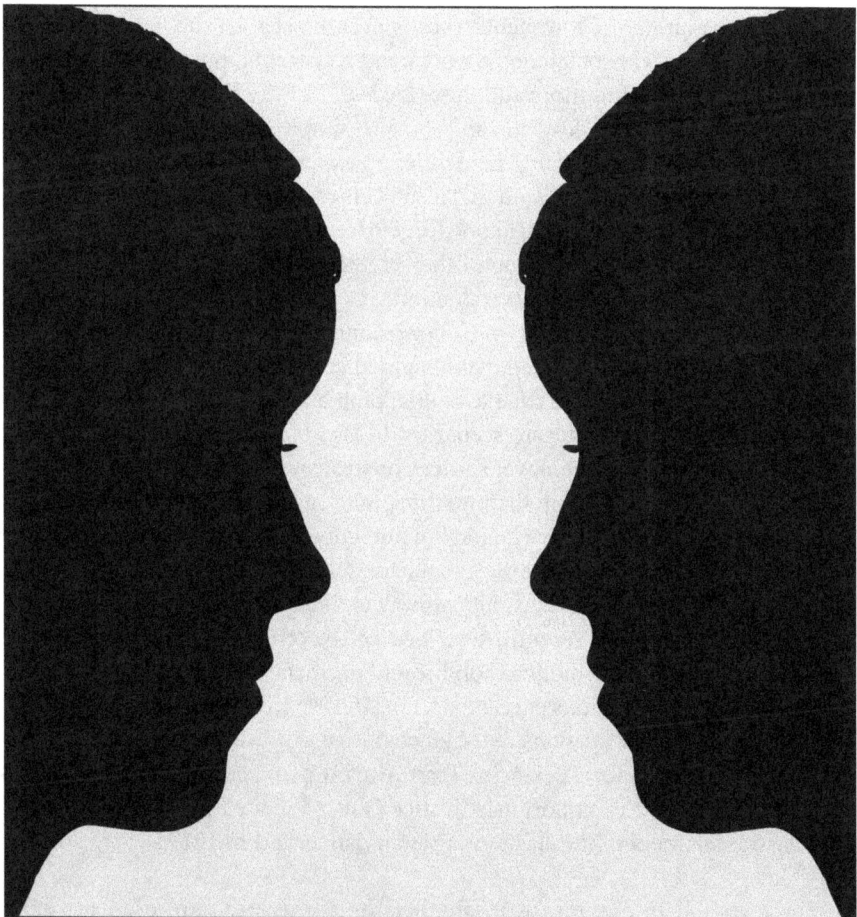

Figure 9.1. Rubin's vase. Artwork by Nevit Dilmen.
Reproduced under a CC BY-SA 3.0 license.

Intellectual growth is developed through what are known as *schemas*, or subcategories of people, social situations, self, and events. People learn information more readily if it fits within their schema, and schemas allows humans to think quickly as they interpret new information—even though they may develop a distorted view of the information.[13,15]

The internet has done much the same with beliefs we call *internet cognitive isoforms*, defined here as a piece of information learned online that is used to connect the "cognitive dots."

Social media, like the Gestalt concept of an optical illusion, allows for the rapid intake of information which, through cognitive shortcuts, saves brain energy. We all have a basic understanding of how social media works. Internet users frequently encounter messages, posts, and the responses to them. If a post on Facebook or Instagram gathers a lot of measurable clicks, shares, or likes, that post will be more visible in news feeds. Items advocating hatred and bigotry, conspiracy theories, or COVID-19 health misinformation generate reactions—both positive and negative. A false post about the danger of vaccines may generate a huge number of comments, mostly arguing against the post—but due to algorithms in the way social media works, the very fact of high engagement levels drives the odd post into more and more feeds.[16] Such feedback mechanisms, also called echo-chambers,[17] lead to rapid binary, simplistic, and absolute thinking. In a 2015 study at Yale utilizing nine different experiments with more than 1,000 participants, psychologists found that if subjects received information through internet searches, they rated their knowledge base as much greater than those who obtained the information through other methods such as reading a text. Thus, people *feel* smarter when they search online.[18]

In a 2023 study at University College London, an online experiment with nearly 600 people demonstrated that imagined and perceived stimuli can become intermixed in people's minds due to overlapping brain circuits. Professor Stephen Fleming wrote, "In near-future scenarios, in which brain stimulation or virtual reality technology become novel sources of strong sensory signals, our findings imply it may be more difficult than we think to tell apart reality and unreality."[19(np)] This helps us understand how contagion and copycat effects can happen quickly in online subcultures, something lone-actor terrorism researchers Reid Meloy and Jeffrey Pollard described as the "runway to violence."[20]

Harvard psychiatrists recently described anti-vaccination conspiracy theories, which are frequently encountered online and on social media platforms, as EOBs that place large populations at risk for COVID-19.[21] In a world with nuclear, biological, and chemical weapons, internet cognitive isoforms could easily present a clear and present danger. Balancing First Amendment speech protection against these threats is of dire importance. Justice Oliver Wendell Holmes, Jr. delivered the classic statement of the clear and present danger test in 1919:

> The question in every case is whether the words used are used in such circumstances and are of such a nature as to create a clear and present danger that they will bring about the substantive evils that Congress has a

right to prevent. It is a question of proximity and degree. When a nation is at war many things that might be said in time of peace are such a hindrance to its effort that their utterance will not be endured so long as men fight, and that no court could regard them as protected by any constitutional right.[22(p52)]

For example, an internet cognitive isoform that purported a "nuclear attack" between Russia and NATO could spawn an actual nuclear attack.[23]

UNDERSTANDING THE BINARY BIAS

Humans assess large sets of evidence first by simplifying and internally summarizing it. One of the main ways we do that is to boil the information down to a limited number of categories, usually two. Say you're trying to assess the health effects of three cups of coffee per day. You'll find that most recent research says that three will do good, but six may be harmful. It's natural for the mind to summarize the research into two categories—drinking coffee is good for you, or drinking coffee is bad for you.

Jumping to conclusions without carefully analyzing the data available is a feature of human cognition. A 2018 study[24] by researchers at Carnegie Mellon and Yale Universities demonstrated that we suffer from a "binary bias" when it comes to understanding evidence—we have a "tendency to impose categorical distinctions on continuous data,"[24(p1846)] and to "treat evidence as all or none without tracking the differential impact of graded evidence."[24(p1848)] In nine studies looking at evidence assessment in several contexts, the researchers documented this bias, concluding that it applies not just in evaluating statistics and other technical contexts, but also in a wide variety of other social judgments relating to finance, health, public policy, and law.

For instance, binary bias can come into play when it comes to a witness's performance on the stand. Jurors are likely to judge the witness either as "bad" or "good"—no in-between. The good ones are credible and useful, and the bad ones have some weakness—and maybe it is just one thing—that undermines their credibility. On the other hand, an attorney may actually take advantage of the binary bias in trying to win a case. For example, stripping away the complexities of medical decision-making and the standard of care in a medical malpractice suit, it is simply easier to think of a physician's actions as being either "safe" or "unsafe." There are evolutionary causes for this kind of thinking, the authors of this study claim. "The root of the binary bias may lie in behavioral control. Many critical behavioral outputs such as fight versus flight and sustenance versus poison are go/no-go (binary) decisions. These survival-relevant processes may shape the sorts of lower-level judgments made in the current studies."[24(p1856)] In other words, sometimes our very survival depends on being able to make a decision between two courses of action quickly—and our brains are less effective at weighing all of the options and nuances.

In the last analysis, cognitive shortcuts, a phenomenon pioneered by Daniel Kahneman, allow us to process an otherwise overwhelming amount of information—and where better than the internet to find overwhelming amounts of information? Binary bias affects how we understand and interpret data, and alters decision-making. This bias affects not only explicit judgments but also how implicit attitudes (such as racial prejudices) are updated on the basis of new evidence. Thus, the binary bias appears to be a pervasive aspect of cognition with extensive real-world implications—including the online contagion seen in targeted attacks.

DON'T TREAD ON ME

Psychologist Solomon Asch strengthened the connection between the Gestalt perspective[8] and social psychology in his powerful seminal research on group effects.[25,26] In Asch's conformity experiments, a group of volunteers were shown a card with a line on it. They were next shown another card with three lines of different lengths on it, and a volunteer was asked to match the first card's line length with one of the three lines on the second card. It was a simple task that volunteers were told was a vision test. However, when a group of planted individuals (party to the aims of the experiment) told the subjects that a nonmatching line was the same length, people conformed—despite their better judgment. The study found that group size influenced whether subjects conformed with the views of the group, even if they could see that those views were wrong. The bigger the majority group, the more people conformed, but only up to a certain point.

Asch's 1952 study could not be more relevant today. On social media, the more "views" or "likes" (thumbs ups, hearts) that a social media post receives, the more it is believed—even if it is wrong—allowing the growth and nurturance of internet cognitive isoforms. If tens of thousands of people agree that vaccination is dangerous, how could that be wrong? And yet it is. The effect is especially strong if shared by someone the user knows and respects—or thinks they know, such as a celebrity. This cognitive illusion can be weaponized during political movements or terrorist recruitment efforts. Treading on moral codes becomes a matter worth fighting for and even dying for, the cognitive fuel for individuals who harbor EOBs. One US military symbol of this is the Gadsden rattlesnake flag, which reads "Don't Tread on Me." The flag has more recently been hijacked by extremists as a symbol of anti-government militias.[27]

Changes in thinking and emotion have been found to be an important correlate in lone-actor radicalization and threat assessment.[28] Evidence from neuroscience establishes many interactions among cognition and emotions (anger, contempt, and disgust), as contributors to motivation in violent psychopathology[29] Contempt contains a moral component, in which one looks down on another from a position of superiority or judgment for being less than or less equal to, or inferior.

EMOTIONAL TAGGING

One internet propaganda meme that became popular during the run-up to the 2016 presidential election featured various photos of colorful candies[30]; in one version was the text: "Here are 10,000 M&Ms for you, ten or so have been poisoned and there is no way to tell which ones. Do you still want them? No? Now you understand why I don't think we should be letting refugee immigrants here."

This meme illustrates the internet cognitive isoform concept. Dangerous threats are presented alongside and equated with immigrants in a single seemingly harmless graphic, connecting the dots between them for susceptible viewers. Similar to the faces or vase figure, the brain processes new information using previously learned information—poison is dangerous, and immigrants are like poison.

This meme also uses a classical conditioning behavior model, where the unconditioned stimulus (poison candy) is paired with a previously neutral stimulus (immigrants), rendering the latter now dangerous, too. The emotion generated for those who agree with the sentiment against immigrants will fuel the meme's spread to others. It is critical to note that certain assumptions, as well as the abandonment of a certain measure of reason and lack of counter-messaging, are required for logic to flow in the direction of EOBs. An individual with an established anti-immigrant schema is more likely to move toward refinement and troubling behavior in its service. That is why one person literally sees or believes something that another person does not (one sees a vase, the other faces).

In general, emotions have important relevance for survival because emotional stimuli tend to capture our attention more easily than non-emotional stimuli. Seeing and detecting potential threats, like a poisonous snake or spider, and remembering where they are located are important survival functions. Advertisers have discovered, for instance, that incorporating imagery such as spiders can draw attention to their products. In one scientific experiment, people were more likely to locate snakes or spiders in photographs in grid-pattern arrays compared to fear-irrelevant pictures belonging to the same category, like flowers or mushrooms.[31] Newly acquired information about threats (spiders, snakes, immigrants) and their location becomes quickly communicated to others—now more than ever, thanks to the internet and social media.

The emotions of anger, contempt, and disgust (toward bugs or, in our example, immigrants) also fuel violent rhetoric. As we have seen, examples abound of these emotions in targeted attacks. Consider Nazi propaganda chief Joseph Goebbels, who stated, "A Jew for me is an object of disgust. I feel like vomiting when I see one. Christ could not possibly have been a Jew. It is not necessary to prove that scientifically—it is a fact. I do not need to prove this with science or scholarship. It is so!"[32(p100)] Elliot Rodger, a misogynistic killer of seven people, stated, "Humanity is a disgusting, wretched, depraved and evil species."[33(p79)] He later became a hero for the incel (involuntarily celibate) subculture online. The emotion imbuing these beliefs acts as an accelerant, spreading them far and wide. As Reid Meloy first noted, emotions such as contempt and disgust, in particular, advance the fantasy of ambient purification (morally reasoned cleansing of the environment—think of the Nazis' Final Solution), and the fantasy of ushering in a destined utopia.[34] Further, they enable the grandiose fantasy of becoming a pseudocommando, warrior, or martyr for a cause.[28]

Let's look at some other cases in which moral codes, as well as emotional tagging and cognitive isoforms, resulted in targeted attacks.

In 1692, the daughter and niece of Samuel Parris, a minister of Salem Village in what would one day become Massachusetts, began having violent contortions and uncontrollable screaming fits. Nine-year-old Elizabeth (Betty) Parris and 11-year-old Abigail Williams, as well as other girls in Salem, were diagnosed as having "bewitchment." Assumptions about witches were common in this century, thus allowing the development of the EOB that these young women were witches. Arrest warrants were issued for those whom the girls claimed had bewitched them—a slave, Tituba, along with two other women, one homeless and the other a beggar. Horrific tests that were meant to reveal whether one was a witch included stripping, hog-tying of hands and feet, and being thrown into a pond to see if they sank or floated. Witches were thought to have rejected the sacrament of baptism, and as such that the water would reject their souls and force them to float, while an innocent person would just sink. Some drowned before they could be hoisted out.

In another test, the accused witch had to recite the Lord's Prayer flawlessly (no repeating after errors). Jane Wenham was accused of being a witch because she stumbled during her recitation. George Burroughs, a convicted witch, recited the prayer flawlessly before he was hanged. His ability to recite it was dismissed as trickery by the devil (rejection of countervailing evidence). In 1662, Rose Cullender and Amy Denny were charged with bewitching two girls. The girls had seizures in which they would clench their fists tightly, and their fists could not be pried apart. However, when either of the accused women touched the girls, their hands opened. When blindfolded and touched by others, the girls also opened their fists, but the two women were hung as witches anyway.[35,36] The flow of logic in this case is:

> Prior assumptions about witches (schema) → anger, contempt and disgust
> → extreme overvalued belief → cleansing of witches in Salem.

JINNS, DEMONS, AND EVIL EYE

In the early morning hours of July 8, 2009, paramedics were summoned to a home in Birmingham, United Kingdom. In the bedroom they discovered a dead

21-year-old woman who was six months pregnant. Her name was Naila Mumtaz, a recent immigrant to the United Kingdom from Pakistan. The paramedics attempted unsuccessfully to revive her. Her family believed she had been possessed by a Jinn (genie), which they tried to remove by smothering her. Mumtaz's husband, his parents, and her brother-in-law were all found guilty of murder by the Birmingham Crown Court and received prison sentences.[37] Similar to the Mumtaz case is that of the brutal killing of a four-year-old in rural Missouri. She had been subjected to beatings and extreme cold water in a pond at the hands of her family and neighbors in an alleged effort to remove a demon from her body.[38] In 2007, a 22-year-old drowned and a 14-year-old was severely injured during a Maori exorcism in New Zealand.[39] Exorcism rituals, which depend utterly on extreme beliefs, can include restraining, beating, or suffocating a person, and can turn deadly. Such rituals occur in many countries.

As highlighted by these cases, EOBs in possession or demonic influence are not psychotic or delusional disorders—a group of people worked together to murder these individuals. Not all people develop such beliefs, as certain assumptions and preexisting predispositions are required to develop such newly acquired cognitive isoforms. Thus, shared beliefs and their accompanying assumptions can bring a cruel and determined ruling passion in which alternatives to violence are no longer contemplated.[40] Many problems encountered by psychiatrists and courts worldwide are rooted in such shared belief systems relating to abnormal illness behavior (once called *hysteria*). These can include mesmerism, witch hunters, the evil eye, Jinn (genie) possession, demonic possession, astrology, and other invisible forces.[41]

In Jewish mysticism, a *dybbuk* (Yiddish for "cling") is the wandering soul of a dead person that comes to possess living people. Evil eye, Jinn, or devil possession as a source of human illness is a commonly encountered issue in the Middle East and Asia. Pseudo-symptoms are prominent in these cases. One exorcist in East London reportedly surrounds himself with Korans, olive oil, and a spray bottle that he uses on clients possessed by Jinns. He believes that some people have unnecessary treatment and surgeries because the Jinn has "tricked doctors."[42]

Many British Pakistanis attribute their physical and psychological problems to Jinn. They commonly believe in black magic or evil eye. Some wear a blue medallion with the figure of an eye to ward off evil spirits. There have been numerous cases in which a person delayed or refused medical care due to the belief that the illness was caused by Jinn. Patients who are highly suggestable can fall victim to pseudo-beliefs, and occasionally experience spontaneous recovery (a conversion disorder). Here the flow toward an EOB is:

> Assumptions about Jinns or devil (schema) → anger, contempt and disgust → extreme overvalued belief → cleansing of "evil."

From cases such as these, we can see that a logical progression occurs between the emergence of EOBs, brain plasticity and a targeted attack. This is best understood through the lens of the individual and his subcultural background and surroundings. Subcultures contain important assumptions (schemas); emotions of anger, contempt, humiliation, and disgust are accelerants for EOBs; an ambient purification (cleansing) is then seen as a morally sanctioned reason for killing.

10

Suicide

A Collective Identity

> *Overvalued ideas are experienced by the patient as normal and justified, fully explained by the events that led to their formation.*
> —CARL WERNICKE[1]

Many mass shootings and acts of terrorism or assassinations involve overt acts of suicide, or at least a high risk of being killed during an attack. Most scientists that study suicide are intently focused on causes of suicide such as mental illness, substance use, interpersonal relationships, and so on. What remains a challenge is to determine the relationship between violence toward others (terrorism) and violence toward self (suicide). Consensus among terrorism experts, notably Jerold Post, is that the notion of a "collective identity" may best explain it. Social psychology and group dynamics help explain the "normality" of, and absence of individual psychopathology in, suicide bombers. Thus, as we shall further explore in this chapter, some suicides can be seen as part of the "collective identity" of a subculture. Subcultures vary with epochs in politics, religion, and shifting online subcultures. Familiar examples include *seppuku*, kamikaze suicidal pilots, the 9/11 attacks, some U.S. mass shooters, and Palestinian suicide bombers—each epoch determined by the context of a unique, shared, and often time-limited social climate. While many factors contribute to suicide, the historical examples presented here represent compelling reasons why we must continue to develop new hypotheses and to collect more data on this topic.

The Japanese concept of *seppuku* dates back many centuries and is a form of suicide by disembowelment. It was part of the samurai code of honor and was also used to restore honor during earlier epochs in Japanese history. For example, after World War II, some soldiers and civilians chose to die rather than surrender to U.S. forces.

A recent and vivid example of suicide embedded in Japanese culture is that of Yukio Mishima, an important 20th-century Japanese author and a controversial figure. His political leanings included a spirited pride in Japanese culture and an opposition to postwar democracy, globalism, and communism. He also was alarmed by what he thought of as "radical left" ideologies, especially among college students. On November 25, 1970, Mishima submitted the last installment of *The Sea of Fertility*, his four-volume epic on Japanese life, considered his greatest work, to his publisher. He and some followers then proceeded to a military building in Tokyo and seized control of a general's office. From there Mishima gave a speech to about 1,000 assembled servicemen, urging them to overthrow Japan's constitution, which forbids Japanese rearmament. The soldiers were not swayed by his extreme beliefs, and Mishima committed *seppuku* (ritual suicide) by disemboweling himself with his sword.[2]

The psychology behind Mishima's ritual suicide was spirited—rooted in narcissism[3] and based on a traditional moral code of honor and allegiance to the emperor. The degree to which he actually believed what he espoused will never be known, particularly in light of Western influences that played a major role in his worldwide success. A lifelong and public fixation with ritual *seppuku* virtually demanded that Mishima follow through with his calculated final act. Perhaps ironically, failure to follow through after years of apparent fascination with the practice might have resulted in shame, warranting a less-than-noble suicide. His belief in a moral code from times past, and in the power of shame, appears to have been equally extreme and overvalued.

Mishima was a child during World War II, when suicide served as a weapon of war in the form of determined kamikaze pilots. On the surface it would seem that an overvalued belief in devotion and sacrifice to the emperor played the leading role in kamikaze mentality. Fealty to one's leader was a time-honored tradition in Japan. But loyalty and obedience were not the only factors that may have influenced kamikaze pilots.

Unlikely as it may seem, a number of Japanese kamikaze pilots did survive the war.[4,5] One such pilot was Kenichiro Oonuki, who was interviewed for a *BBC* documentary by Laurence Rees.[5] According to Oonuki, all pilots had been instructed to return to base if their planes developed a fault on the way to their targets. In April 1945, while en route to attack the American fleet off the island of Okinawa, Oonuki had been forced to land his plane—stuffed with explosives—because of engine trouble. He was rescued by the Japanese navy and interrogated about the failure of his mission. Shortly after this, the war in the Pacific ended.

Oonuki stated later that survival had given him "a sense of a burden."[5,np] He knew he was not supposed to be alive to tell his story 60 years after the end of the war. His duty was to smash his plane into the superstructure of an American warship. But his survival meant that he was able to correct the central myth of the kamikaze—that these young pilots all went to their deaths willingly, enthused by the samurai spirit.

On the contrary, Oonuki said, when he and his fighter pilot colleagues were first asked to volunteer for this "special attack mission," they thought the whole idea "ridiculous." But given the night to think about their decision, the men reconsidered. They feared that if they did not volunteer, their families would be ostracized and their parents told that their sons were cowards, "not honorable, shameful." Then they would be sent to the most dangerous part of the front line where they would surely still die—but dishonored. As a result, Oonuki stated, "Everyone put down the answer which was opposite from what we were feeling. Probably it's unthinkable in the current days of peace. Nobody wanted to, but everybody said, 'Yes, [I volunteer] with all my heart.' That was the surrounding atmosphere. We could not resist."[5,np]

When it was time for his squadron to depart, Oonuki learned that his plane had a mechanical defect and that he could not leave with the pilots he had trained with.

I went to my colleagues, once their engines had started and they were on the runway. The azaleas were in full bloom, and so I made a bouquet of azaleas and gave it to my pilot comrades. And one comrade said, "I am going ahead of you. I wanted to meet my destiny with you. I'm sorry." They were the saddest eyes I ever saw. It's often said that before one's death a person has that really sad expression in their eyes, like a deep-sea fish looking up at the blue sky above.[5,np]

Oonuki left the next day, intending to meet his death with another group of kamikaze pilots, but his plane never reached the American fleet—his life saved by an unreliable engine.

Thus, while spirited devotion to a living god in the form of the emperor did appear to inspire many to suicide, for others the fear of shame (their own, or that of their loved ones) proved to be more compelling than the fear of death. Whichever path these men took, like Mishima, an extreme and overvalued system of belief set their course. Oonuki warned that in a time of crisis, as during the Second World War, "you are drawn into this major vortex and swirl around without your own will."[5,np] He well understood the concept of extreme overvalued beliefs (EOBs)—by comparing some kamikazes to Al-Qaeda terrorists after the 9/11 atttacks.[4]

THE 9/11 ATTACKS, MARTYRDOM, AND SUICIDE

On September 11, 2001, nearly 3,000 people perished in the deadliest terrorist attack in U.S. history. The attacks were a series of coordinated hijacked passenger jets perpetrated by 19 determined Al-Qaeda terrorists and masterminded by Osama bin Laden. His second in command and operational leader was Ayman al-Zawahiri, an eye surgeon who founded the Egyptian Islamic Jihad terrorist group. Zawahiri was part of a militant Islamic group that assassinated President Anwar Sadat for making a peace deal with Israel. He proclaimed that his goal was to establish an Islamic state. Bin Laden and Zawahiri espoused many anti-Semitic and anti-Western beliefs. Much has been written about the extremist motives for the attacks; however, the attacks also involved suicide. The hijackers' predominant

EOB was that U.S. foreign policy had oppressed, killed, and harmed Muslims in the Middle East. Bin Laden's moral justification can be detected in some of his rhetoric:

> What the United States tastes today is a very small thing compared what we have tasted for tens of years. Our nation has been tasting this humiliation and contempt for more than 80 years. Its sons are being killed, its blood is being shed, its holy lands are being attacked, and it is not being ruled according to what God has decreed. Despite this, nobody cares.[6(p107)]

Bin Laden subscribed to a literal interpretation of Islam, including Sharia law. With a spirited and charismatic charm, he called upon the West to convert to Islam and reject immorality. In 1998, he and Zawahiri co-signed a fatwa in the name of the World Islamic Front for jihad against Jews and Christians, declaring that "it is the duty of every Muslim to liberate the al-Aqsa Mosque in Jerusalem and the holy mosque in Mecca from their grip." Muhammad Atta, the leader of the 9/11 terrorist cell, urged the hijackers to "crave death and to be optimistic."[7(p1)] He also wrote, "the virgins are calling you,"[8(p1)] a reference to the terrorists' belief that Muslim martyrs will ascend to paradise and marry 72 black-eyed virgins—despite the fact that the designation *shaheed* (martyr) is supposed to be bestowed on Muslims by God, and not by fellow human beings.

Reid Meloy applied psychoanalytic theory to describe the fear of and desire for sexual pleasure and their connection with the purported rewards of martyrdom.[9] The term *shaheed* (martyr) is considered one whose place in Paradise is promised, as Atta referenced. In fact, a failure of sexually intimate pair bonding is one of the distal characteristics of the *Terrorist Radicalization and Assessment Protocol*,[10] and it is possible that promises of sexual gratification after death were especially alluring to some of these impressionable young men.

As seen with this attack and in Mishima's *seppuku*, individuals committing suicide can think rationally, but they do so within the limits of belief systems that are irrational to outsiders—rigid, simplistic, and defended with great emotional intensity. As psychiatrist and CIA analyst Jerrold Post (2001) observed:

> Considering the diversity of causes to which terrorists are committed, the uniformity of their rhetoric is striking. Polarizing and absolutist, it is a rhetoric of "us vs them." It is rhetoric without nuance, without shades of gray. "They," the establishment, are the source of all evil in vivid contrast to "us," the freedom fighters, consumed by righteous rage. And, if "they" are the source of our problems, it follows ineluctably in the special psychologic of the terrorist, that "they" must be destroyed. It is the only just and moral thing to do. Once one accepts the basic premises, the logic reasoning is flawless.[11(p98)]

The collective beliefs of terrorists are relished, amplified, and defended by their possessors. They are simplistic and immutable. Over time, the belief grows more dominant, more refined, and more resistant to challenge. Individuals belonging to

Al-Qaeda have an intense emotional commitment to their beliefs and are willing, eager even, to carry out morally reasoned and spirited violent (and suicidal) behavior in their service.[12] Collateral damage, including the deaths of innocent bystanders, has no meaning or impact.

Suicide is a serious public health concern that, similar to mass shootings and in contrast to popular belief, is not always attributable to a mental illness. It is clear from epidemiological data that individuals suffering from various mental disorders do have an elevated risk of suicide attempts: schizophrenia (9%–15%), depression (25%–50%), alcoholism (13%–50%), and personality disorders (1%–19%)[9]—but many people who complete suicide are determined posthumously to have had no formal diagnosis.[13] As far as pathological fixations are concerned, people with obsessions and delusions have been shown to have an elevated risk of suicide, particularly when co-occurring symptoms of depression and psychosis are present. A history of suicide attempts is the best predictor for future attempts. Common also to those who take their own lives tend to be feelings of worthlessness, hopelessness, despair, and isolation.[14–18]

Despite an enormous body of research on the biological causes of suicide, little has been accomplished in the way of improving this dire public health problem. The mental health community's record of predicting who may attempt suicide is poor.[15,16] Heritability estimates indicate that diagnosed mental disorders do not fully explain the genetic transmission of suicide attempts.[15] Billions of dollars' worth of research and genetic and brain imaging studies have yet to yield a clinically useful biomarker tool in this endeavor.

There have been some advances. Among others, one important development is the Columbia–Suicide Severity Rating Scale,[17] which has been widely adopted to assess and classify suicidality. It is a short questionnaire that requires no formal mental health training and can be administered to individuals of all ages. Overall, it is clear that psychological factors, including group collective identities, and not just biological ones, should be explored as a major contributor to this problem.[16]

SUICIDALITY AND SUBCULTURES

Exploring Wernicke's work,[1] we might now ask, what if an openness to suicide could be construed as an overvalued (and shared) belief, and could it be a key cognitive-affective driver in suicide? For this discussion, we will consider suicidal behavior as its *own* subculture. This may help us understand why all cases of suicide are not explainable according to a DSM-5 diagnosis of major mental disorder, and how subcultures, forming collective "suicidal identities," might influence those who do take their lives, or attempt to do so.[16]

While Emil Durkheim[18] was the first to invoke the idea that social circumstances were of primary importance in suicide, many modern scholars have also weighed in on this issue. Writer and psychologist Kay Redfield Jamison in her book *Night Falls Fast: Understanding Suicide*, discusses the possibility that shared beliefs contribute to its causality.[19] She identifies an important paradoxical effect when using educational media to present case histories of adolescents who have attempted or completed suicide. The intended purpose may be to teach students how to identify who may be at risk for suicidal behavior. However, Jamison argues, the method may also cause some to closely identify with the problems portrayed by the case examples, and such individuals may come to see suicide as the logical solution to their own problems.[19] Professor Thomas Joiner, author of *Why People Die by Suicide*,[20] has described an interpersonal theory of suicide with emphasis on belongingness and perceived burdensomeness, both of which can be thought of as cultural expectations.[16] Thus shared ideologies, along with conditions that might dampen higher brain function from defects in emotion, cognition, and motivation, may be important interactions to consider.[21] Overall, a person-centered focus is imperative.

Returning to Carl Wernicke's work, in his seminal 1906 volume *Grundriss der Psychiatrie in klinischen Vorlesungen*[1] he discussed suicide as a behavior that can be motivated by overvalued ideas. He went further to identify three major life events that commonly precede suicides[22]:

- The death of a loved one;
- The loss of a fortune; and
- Being sentenced to dishonorable punishment.

The motivations behind this subset of suicides might be best described according to the current DSM-5 diagnosis of adjustment disorder.[23] This condition is characterized by the development of emotional or behavioral symptoms in response to an identifiable stressor, with marked distress that is out of proportion to the severity or intensity of the stressor, taking into account the external context and the cultural factors that might influence symptom severity and presentation.[23(p287)] Thus, Wernicke's description of overvalued idea in these examples illustrates an important cognitive-affective driver of a shared, emotional reaction (a distinct subculture) to various types of losses, but which is also pathological when it involves the ultimate decision to commit suicide. For example, a person who has always believed culturally that "old, sick people are just a burden on society" might believe that suicide is an option for him. Another may have been told, "If anything happens to my spouse, I will kill myself." Such beliefs can be viewed as emblematic of certain subcultures.[16]

SUICIDE AFTER THE DEATH OF A LOVED ONE

Contemplating suicide after the death of a loved one is not uncommon. As feelings of unreality set in, the mind may dissociate from the event, resulting in depersonalization, or a loss of the sense of self. Sometimes suicide may seem to be the only alternative to losing one's mind from grief.

U.S. president Joe Biden thought about suicide when his wife Neilia and 13-month-old daughter Amy died in a horrific car crash in 1972. Biden later told of crippling grief and suicidal thoughts, "I thought about it, not doing it. I thought about what it would be like just to go to the Delaware Memorial Bridge and just jump off and end it all." He went on to recount, "But I didn't ever get in the car and do it or wasn't ever even close. What saved me was really my boys."[24(np)]

The loss of a loved one, as Wernicke posited, poses a real threat of suicide. In fact, epidemiologic evidence reveals that one's suicide risk dramatically increases when someone close dies. In a large Finnish study of married persons, an excess mortality from suicide was observed in both men and women who had experienced a loss of a spouse through an accident or violent means.[25] Losing a parent to suicide makes children more likely to die by suicide themselves.[26] Another European study found that the death of a child (particularly when unexpected) is associated with an overall increased mortality from suicide in mothers, but not fathers.[27] The universal emotional reaction, or archetypes, to such losses are shared, and during an individual's darkest moments, can become overvalued, especially in the presence of mental illness and/or substance use.[19] Time, it seems, or the firm belief that suicide is a mortal sin, diminishes the conviction that suicide is the only viable option (a cultural identity effect).

SUICIDE AFTER LOSS OF A FORTUNE

During the final months of 1929, there were news reports of high-profile suicides of those who had lost fortunes in the stock market crash. The previous years had seen large gains in stock prices, much of them propped up through funds purchased on margin.[28] The day after Black Thursday, C. Fred Stewart, a Chicago real estate dealer who had invested in stocks, lost everything. He was found dead after asphyxiating himself with natural gas in his home kitchen. In Kansas City, insurance broker John Schwitzgebel shot himself twice in the chest.[29] These and other suicides were reported in newspaper stories across the country.

The stories were true, but the impact of the stock market crash was also exaggerated in the media, with suicides portrayed erroneously as all having happened immediately after the stock market crash. In fact, as John Kenneth Galbraith wrote in his book *The Great Crash 1929*, the number of suicides in the United States in the months following the stock market drops in 1929 were among the lowest of that year. The suicide rate had been substantially higher during the summer months before the crash. The false reports about Wall Street suicides compelled New York City's chief medical examiner to publicly refute them.[30] As discussed in Chapter 11, the above examples of suicides similarly illustrate the flow of logic with cognitive isoforms and emotional tagging. Few individuals are able to experience the comfort and luxuries provided by vast wealth. However, the intense emotional reaction to losing it can move some individuals to consider suicide due to the (extreme and overvalued) belief that such a loss would be too painful to overcome.

SUICIDE AFTER BEING SENTENCED TO PRISON

Daniel Jorge Correia de Abreu, 29, and Safiro Teixeira Furtado, 28, were killed by gunshots fired into their vehicle. Aaron Hernandez, a tight end for the New England Patriots, was investigated for their murders. In 2013 police also investigated Hernandez for the shooting death of Odin Lloyd, whose body was found in an industrial park, with several gunshot wounds to the back and chest. Hernandez was later arrested and charged with that murder. On April 15, 2015, he was found guilty of murder in the first degree in Lloyd's death. He was sentenced to life in prison without any possibility of parole. In 2017, he was acquitted in the deaths of Abreu and Furtado. However, just five days later, Hernandez was found dead, having hanged himself using a bedsheet that he had attached to his cell window after jamming the cell door so that it could not be opened. An autopsy revealed that he may also have suffered from a degenerative brain disease that might have made him more vulnerable to suicidal ideation.[31]

In another high-profile suicide, the wealthy financier Jeffrey Epstein fatally threw himself off his jail cell's top bunk bed. Epstein had been accused of sexually abusing girls and women over a period of decades; in 2008 federal prosecutors identified 36 people (as young as age 14) whom he had victimized. Epstein entered into a plea deal after serving 13 months in custody (but with extended work release). He was again charged in 2019 for the sex trafficking of minors, but completed suicide before the case could reach trial. This time, the evidence gathered was robust. FBI agents raided his Manhattan townhouse and found evidence of sex trafficking, including thousands of sexually suggestive photographs of women and girls. Conspiracy theories later swirled around the internet, claiming that Epstein had not really killed himself but was assassinated, or that he was still alive on a beach somewhere in the Middle East.[32]

Studies show that suicide is the second leading cause of death in jails (heart disease is first). Hanging is the most common method (bedsheets are easily accessible). Those charged with violent offenses such as kidnapping, rape, or homicide have up to a five times greater suicide rate compared to nonviolent offenders. About 12% of the suicides occur in the first 24 hours of incarceration.[33] As Wernicke noted, offenders often consider their situation as "dishonorable punishment."[1] The act of suicide in such a dire situation, in which one's freedom is lost, can be seen as framed by an ideology—"If I have to go to prison, I would rather be dead." Such suicides can often lead to lawsuits against jail personnel and the mental health professionals that evaluate the incarcerated, placing blame on staff for not taking appropriate suicidal precautions.

SUICIDE CONTAGION

Let's further consider suicide as a form of ideological framing and overvalued belief in American culture. Seattle in the 1980s is considered by many to be the birthplace of a popular genre of music known as grunge—a heavy metal sound with a punk rock edge. Loose plaid shirts, ripped jeans and sandals were the style's edgy look. Bands such as *Nirvana, Pearl Jam, Stone Temple Pilots, Alice in Chains,* and *Soundgarden* sold many hit albums from the mid-1980s well into the 1990s. The lyrics often centered around suicide, and highlighted many psychological issues as well as liberating themes. *Nirvana* lead singer Kurt Cobain famously died in 1994 by a self-inflicted gunshot wound to the head. He was just 27 years old. *Soundgarden* singer Chris Cornell followed in 2017. Cornell's close friend Chester Bennington, of the band *Linkin Park*, then killed himself on Cornell's birthday. The two suicides occurred in a very similar manner, by hanging. Tragically, an increase in suicides by adolescent fans was observed in the wake of Bennington's death, with young people often utilizing similar methods.[34]

Suicide contagion was also observed after the deaths of Marilyn Monroe and comedian/actor Robin Williams.[35,36] This is referred to as a suicide *mass cluster*.[35] Kay Redfield Jamison notes that places and methods can become "suicide magnets."[19] For instance, if a local newspaper reports that a certain mountain cliff has been the site of several recent suicides, others may be drawn to it—unless the newspaper is careful about how the story is presented. Another type of clustering, called *point clusters*, have also been identified in several schools and communities in which an outbreak of suicide can take several lives within a short time span.[37] In 2019, suicide was the second leading cause of death for people between the ages of 10 and 34 (unintentional injury was the first).[38]

There are also many examples throughout history of mass suicides, often under the leadership of individuals with spirited and charismatic—yet deadly—charms. Such EOBs were the cognitive driver behind the mass suicide of 909 inhabitants (including 304 children) of Jonestown, Guyana, from cyanide poisoning in 1978. Reverend Jim Jones, founder of the People's Temple, instructed his followers to commit suicide while spreading rigidly held conspiracy theories concerning intelligence organizations that were thought to be conspiring against their temple. Similarly, 39 followers of the Heaven's Gate cult died in a mass suicide in California in 1999. They held rigid nondelusional beliefs that their suicides would allow them to exit their "human vessels," allowing their souls to go on a journey aboard a spaceship they believed to be following comet Hale-Bopp. Some men in the group underwent castration in preparation for their "afterlives." The Aum Shinrikyo cult attacked a Tokyo subway with sarin nerve gas in 1995, killing nearly a dozen people and injuring nearly 5,000. The Movement for the Restoration of the Ten Commandments of God was a "doomsday cult" religious movement in which 778 people perished in a series of poisonings and killings; these deaths could be considered either suicide or mass murder perpetrated by group leaders owing to belief in an approaching apocalypse.[39] It should not be a surprise that such suicidal contagion could occur in an online world, often detached from the face-to-face grounding of contact with other humans.

ONLINE SUICIDE SUBCULTURES

Since the dawn of the internet age, suicide rates among adolescents and young adults have drastically increased—leaving cause and effect an open question. Suicide is now the tenth leading cause of death in the United States and the second leading cause for adults age 10–24.[40] Underlying schemas, such as perceived parental bonding, social isolation, shame, and abandonment may be important to consider.[41] In one British case, 14-year-old Molly Russell saved 2,100 images linked to depression and suicide before taking her own life in 2017. A Meta Instagram executive apologized after a coroner's inquest revealed the viewed images in London.[42]

In 2020, another 14-year-old teenager, this time in the United States, was found dead after hanging herself. Her parents found a simulated "hanging video" on her phone. Apparently it had circulated widely, before Instagram removed it. The parents are now suing, particularly since the discovery of a large trove of internal data leaked by whistleblowers, demonstrating the profoundly negative impact of this disturbing "collective identity" in teenagers.[43] There are now more than 1,200 families pursuing lawsuits against social media companies including TikTok, Snapchat, YouTube, Roblox, and Meta, the parent company to Instagram and Facebook, for various mental health–related issues, including suicide and eating disorders.[44]

As far as empirical data, tweets have been studied to determine whether exposure to prominent and sensationalized news stories is associated with suicide risk. Investigators at the University of Toronto noted that tweets presenting suicide deaths, as well as sensationalized news stories about suicide and ones that describe society as "not doing enough" to prevent them, were associated with higher risk.[45] These and other studies[46] suggest that social media subcultures may be important to consider in the recent observed increase in suicide rates among young adults and teens, but some online material may also be protective.[40]

It seems apparent that suicide can be driven by pathological fixations, including EOBs which, as they are shared, become refined and increasingly binary, simplistic, and absolute. Higher reasoning and brain function may have become dampened by predisposing factors, but this can happen to those with a healthy and functioning brain, too. This may be important not only when analyzing cases of violence from acts of terrorism, but also in more universal suicide-prevention efforts. Further research into suicides utilizing Wernicke's description of fixations and the role of schemas is needed to explore this phenomenon.

11

Extreme Overvalued Beliefs in Literature

While it is often stated that art reflects life, the reverse is also true. Throughout the centuries, works of fiction, in books or on stage, have focused on characters whose actions, under numerous guises, cannot be explained other than through the concept of extreme overvalued beliefs. The following examples are but a sampling of all that can be found.

In his original discourse on overvalued ideas, Carl Wernicke[1] chose Dostoyevsky's Rodion Raskolnikov, the protagonist in *Crime and* Punishment,[2] as a primary example to express his delineation from delusions.[1] The novella, published serially in 1866 in a monthly journal called *The Russian Messenger*, allowed Wernicke to explore the moral and psychological dangers of radicalism. Wernicke observed that Rodion Raskolnikov held overvalued ideas as a motive for murder and likely used the story as an example because of its notoriety.[1]

Crime and Punishment is set in St. Petersburg, Russia, where Raskolnikov develops a grandiose belief that intelligent men are above the law. A former law student, he relishes the fantasy of becoming an extraordinary man with special talents to offer the world. However, he has trouble relating to other people, and feels rejected and isolated. As a social misfit, he believes that he is destined to do great things, beyond the mundane existence of those around him: "I simply hinted that an 'extraordinary' man has the right . . . that is not an official right, but an inner right to decide in his own conscience to overstep . . . certain obstacles, and only in case it is essential for the practical fulfillment of his idea (sometimes, perhaps, of benefit to the whole of humanity)."[2(p211)]

The idea that he can even break laws to serve his own lofty goals becomes amplified; his thinking becomes more refined over time and creates a riveting tension for the reader. Raskolnikov's warped moral stance becomes increasingly binary, simplistic, and absolute, culminating in a plan to steal money from an elderly, unscrupulous pawnbroker. However, while in the act of executing his crime, he is surprised to discover the victim is at home. Fearing capture, he finds an axe nearby, quipping, "When reason fails, the devil helps!"[2(p59)] and brutally murders the elderly pawnbroker and her sister, who walks in on them.[2(p59)]

Raskolnikov confesses his crime to Sonia, an impoverished prostitute. He defends his actions, explaining that it wasn't *just* for the victim's money, but rather his grandiose pathway toward redemption: "Yes, that's what it was! I wanted to become Napoleon, that is why I killed her. . . . Do you understand now?"[2(p337)]

Raskolnikov does not literally believe that he will become Napoleon Bonaparte; instead he believes that he can make exceptional contributions to humanity in the way that Napoleon instituted sweeping social and legal reforms in France. Thus he believes that he has the right, even the duty, to break the law, including by committing murder, in pursuit of making "exceptional contributions" to humanity.

Wernicke argued that Raskolnikov was not suffering from a psychotic delusion, but rather from an overvalued idea. Wernicke explains that events, ideas, and coincidences help explain overvalued beliefs, as opposed to abnormalities seen in delusions. Raskolnikov does not suffer other features suggestive of a severe mental disorder such as schizophrenia. In schizophrenia, patients also would typically experience other symptoms such as hallucinations, and gross disorganization of speech and behavior.[1-3] His changes in *thinking and emotion* are not due to an abnormal disease process, but instead are features seen in violent true believers (cognitive rigidity, clandestine excitement, contempt, and disgust).[4,5]

Wernicke sharply distinguished overvalued ideas from delusions, arguing that fixations can usually be identified on clinical grounds. He regarded overvalued ideas as springing from a struggle involving the individual's personality.[1] *Crime and Punishment* provides an enduring legacy of morality related to criminality and has inspired numerous works of literature, film, and television shows. German philosopher Friedrich Nietzsche wrote that Dostoevsky was the only psychologist from whom he had anything to learn.[6]

Overvalued thinking, discussed throughout this book, is commonly seen in assassinations and in lone-actor as well as group terrorism. Indeed, the presence of a belief system that justifies an intent to act, such as a religious belief system, a political philosophy, or a secular commitment, is known as *ideological framing*, and is considered an important characteristic in many acts of targeted violence[7] Ted Kaczynski (the Unabomber), for example, believed that he was saving the Earth from what he regarded as a dire threat posed by technological progress. Members of the terrorist group Al-Qaeda, using passenger airplanes as missiles, believed they were contributing to the moral betterment of the world through their extreme version of Islam. Online followers of QAnon believe that the insurrection at the U.S. Capitol was needed to save the United States from a "tyrannical government."[8,9]

Nietzsche admired Dostoyevsky, and his characterization of Raskolnikov likely influenced the philosopher's well-known theories on the *Übermensch* (overhuman), which appeared in his most famous work, *Thus Spoke Zarathustra*. The *Übermensch* represents a shift from otherworldly Christian values to human ideals grounded in this life. Zarathustra proclaims that the will of the *Übermensch* is to give meaning to life on Earth, and admonishes his audience to ignore those who promise other-worldly fulfillment.[10,11]

Nietzsche's vision of a superior human, above the fray, was in many ways foreshadowed by Raskolnikov. Students of philosophy have come to relish Nietzsche's humanistic concepts in their original context. Unfortunately, perversions of his ideas and terminology came to be exploited during the rise of the Nazi regime in 1930s Germany.[12,13]

The Nazis attempted to incorporate the concept into their ideology by means of taking Nietzsche's figurative form of speech and creating a literal superiority over other ethnicities. After his death, his sister Elisabeth became the curator and editor of Nietzsche's manuscripts. She reworked his unpublished writings to fit her own German nationalist ideology, while often contradicting or obfuscating Nietzsche's stated opinions, which were explicitly opposed to anti-Semitism. Through her published editions, Nietzsche's work became associated with fascism. Fortunately, 20th-century scholars, notably Georges Bataille (*On Nietzsche*), contested this interpretation of his work, and corrected editions of his writings were soon made available.[14]

Raskolnikov's mental life reveals other recently discovered behavioral characteristics and warning signs common among targeted violent offenders: not only is he *fixated* on moral superiority, but he *identifies* as a warrior (like Napoleon) for his cause; he has *changes in thinking and emotion* (strident and simplistic); he *thwarts occupational goals*; and fails to form an *intimate sexual bond*. These are some examples of the 18 warning signs and distal characteristics developed and validated by noted threat-assessment scholar Reid Meloy.[15]

THE DEVILS OF LOUDUN

Sometimes, a thin line exists between superstition and religion. In the Middle Ages, belief in witches, possession, and pacts with the devil were formally incorporated into Catholicism's religious dogma. Encouraging these beliefs, which may or may not have been shared by all of the clergy, better suited the political purposes of the church and those in power. Fear of the presence of evil in day-to-day life neatly supplemented the fear of eternal damnation encouraged by the church.

Belief in witchcraft, sorcery, demonic possession, and brutal countermeasures necessary to eradicate such perceived evils are present in many cultures and have been given literary treatment by numerous authors and playwrights. In 1953, Arthur Miller's *The Crucible*[16] recounted the Salem witch trials, while serving as an allegory for the existing political milieu of McCarthyism—the extreme and pervasive belief that Communists had penetrated American life.

A year earlier, however, the lesser known historical novel *The Devils of Loudun*, by the literary giant Aldous Huxley,[17] recounted a famous case of alleged sorcery and the injustice that resulted, from a historical and highly literate perspective. *The Devils* is particularly interesting because it involves a genuine belief in witchcraft and demonic possession, coupled with possibly *feigned* possession, and religious and civic leaders who exploit both to achieve their own political ambitions.[18] The novel and its 1971 cinematic interpretation, directed by Ken Russell, focuses on Roman Catholic priest Urbain Grandier and a convent of Ursuline nuns who, in the 1630s, allegedly became possessed by demons after Grandier supposedly made a pact with Satan. In the centuries that followed, the drama that unfolded between 1632 and 1634 has provided rich fodder for historians, theologians, and some of the giants of modern psychology. At its heart lies a variety of extreme overvalued beliefs (EOBs) that drew thousands of curiosity seekers to the small French town of Loudun, where exorcisms continued until 1638.[19]

Father Grandier was charming, eloquent, and arrogant, according to Huxley. He was known to have had his way with many of the town's rich widows and allegedly fathered a daughter with the wife of the local prosecutor. Loved by some and hated by others, Grandier was also rumored to have authored a pamphlet that greatly offended the Capuchins and Cardinal Richelieu, the most powerful man in France. The latter, true or not, set in motion a series of accusations and ultimately violence, all rooted in the general population's "collective identity" and belief in sorcery and demonic possession.

In 1632, a group of nuns accused him of having bewitched them, sending the demon Asmodal, among others, to commit evil and lustful acts with them. Huxley argues that the accusations began after Grandier refused to become spiritual director of the convent, unaware that the Mother Superior, Jeanne des Anges, had become fixated on him after having seen him from afar and having heard of his sexual exploits. According to Huxley, Mother Jeanne, enraged by his rejection, instead invited Grandier's archenemy Canon Jean to become director. She then accused Grandier of using black magic to seduce her. The other nuns were gradually caught up in what was later known as "hysteria," and began to make similar accusations.[19-23]

The nuns likely suffered from mass hysteria, or *conversion disorder*. Freud suggested that mass hysteria starts as a way to repress memories or emotional events that are happening in one's environment, but with the repression of the memory the stress is "converted" into a somatic (physical) symptom.[20] The Salem witch incident serves as a classic example, but more recently, in Le Roy, New York, in 2011, 12 teenage girls began experiencing Tourette-like symptoms. Stress, allegedly, was the cause of their tics, verbal outpourings, and involuntary movements.[21] Their behavior mimicked that of the Ursuline nuns.

According to Jungian analyst Craig Stephenson, Carl Jung used his theory of complexes to account for the phenomena of possession:

> Although Freud wrote about group psychology, he did not include any hypothesis about collective factors in his case of [Haitzmann's] demonological neurosis. Significantly, Jung's definition of demonism does include a collective component. For Jung, the possession at Loudun was an epidemic comparable to what he called the "induced collective psychoses of the twentieth

century," and as a result, an interpretation of possession in an individual such as [nun] Jeanne des Anges should take into account not only the possibility of trauma and the activation of repressed contents in the personal unconscious but also the effects of the collective unconscious. Jeanne des Anges's demonological neurosis psychically infected the other Ursulines, polarized Loudun, and drew crowds from across Europe because her possession articulated both a personal repressed conflict and a collective dilemma.[22(p558)]

In his appendix to the novel, Huxley comments on EOBs and the contagious pack mentality known as "herd intoxication" in the case of the Loudun incidents.[17]

When crowd-delirium is exploited for the benefit of governments and orthodox churches, the exploiters are always very careful not to allow the intoxication to go too far. The ruling minorities make use of their subjects' craving for downward self-transcendence in order, first, to amuse and distract them and, second, to get them into a sub-personal state of heightened suggestibility. Religious and political ceremonials are welcomed by the masses as opportunities for getting drunk on herd-poison, and by their rulers as opportunities for planting suggestions in minds which have momentarily ceased to be capable of reason or free will.[17(p319)]

Ultimately, Grandier's torture and death at the stake was the result of several factors: his lecherous behavior, primarily toward the prosecutor's wife; his offending Cardinal Richelieu directly; and his influence on the Ursuline nuns stricken by hysteria and pack mentality. Even under torture and engulfed in the flames of the stake, he denied any guilt to the bitter end.

In the years that followed, pamphlets denouncing Grandier's unjust punishment and accusing the nuns of feigning their possession reinforced the popular final assessment of this tragic, politically motivated atrocity.[23]

MISHIMA'S DRESS REHEARSAL

Yukio Mishima's novels were enormously popular around the world in the 1950s and 1960s, but his views on Japanese politics and ritual suicide, discussed in the previous chapter, were well outside the Western paradigm. His novels only touched infrequently on these issues. The exceptions were the autobiographical *Confessions of a Mask* (1949),[24] which dealt with his childhood and emerging homosexuality, and *Sun and Steel* (1968),[25] which documented the author's fixation on health and extreme bodybuilding.

One of his pieces that adopted a military mindset and did discuss suicide head-on was the 1960 short story "Patriotism,"[26] later made into a movie starring Mishima himself. The story portrays not only extreme political views and romantic love; it also served as a literal dress rehearsal for the extreme final act about which Mishima seems to have fantasized his entire life.

The story is about the 1936 Ni Ni-Roku incident, in which a group of young officers, members of a secret society, attempted to stage a coup d'état. They murdered several cabinet members, contending that their loyalty was to the emperor alone, not corrupt government officials. Army Lieutenant Shinji Takeyama was a member of the society but did not take part in the coup. The other members did not want to implicate him because they knew how much he loved his beautiful new bride, Reiko, and did not want to see them parted.

Days passed, and Takeyama, a member of the palace guard, was summoned to help suppress the rebels, all of whom were his close friends and comrades-in-arms. This placed him in an untenable situation for which there was only one extreme solution—to retain his honor, to demonstrate his loyalty to the emperor and to his friends, he would commit ritual suicide.

Reiko saw the final act coming. While Takeyama was away on his mission, trying to avoid betraying his comrades as best he could, she prepared keepsakes for their relatives. When he returned it was clear that for Reiko, too, ritual suicide, alongside the man she loved above all else, was inevitable. In a final confirmation of life, they made love with a passion they had not known since their wedding night. Then Takeyama took his dagger and committed *seppuku*. Reiko followed. Mishima skillfully illustrated, in fiction and film, the powerful and universal links between love, sex, and devotion strong enough to die for.

Patriotism is a story of extremes. The rebels' belief in the sanctity of the emperor and the corruption of the Japanese government led to violence. Takeyama's loyalty to his comrades extended to sacrificing his own life rather than betraying them. And the couples' extreme devotion to each other, to the degree that neither would live without the other, though tragic, displays the extreme of love and loyalty personified.

Patriotism was not the last, nor even the first, time Mishima would perform his own death. In Yasuzô Masumura's yakuza 1960 film, *Afraid to Die*, his character was shot in the back and expired after an extended time. In 1968, he portrayed a taxidermized human statue meant to embody "beauty cut down in its prime" in Kinji Fukasaku's *Black Lizard*.[27] In 1969, he committed *seppuku* in Hideo Gosha's samurai film, *Hitokiri*. Throughout, Mishima continued to write obsessively, as if racing against his real-life demise.

BAD ROMANCE

Couples dying for love has been a literary theme through the ages. Certainly being "in love" exhibits extreme emotion; it is a sentiment shared by millions and, some would argue, a form of obsessive fixation. Mishima knew well the power of connecting love and death. So did Shakespeare. While *Romeo and Juliet* remain the best-known star-crossed lovers, they weren't the firs.[28]

Ovid's story of Pyramus and Thisbe tells of two young lovers who, forbidden to marry because of family rivalries, whisper their love through cracks in a wall. The lovers decide to escape their families and meet under a mulberry tree. Thisbe arrives at the rendezvous first, and narrowly escapes a lion attack, dropping her veil in the process. When Pyramus arrives and finds the blood-soaked veil, he despairs, believing Thisbe to be dead, and throws himself on his sword; when Thisbe returns to the tragic scene, she does the same.[29]

Shakespeare's well-known play repeats the fatal mistake-cum-suicide theme in elegant language fit for the stage. The young couple marry in secret with the help of Juliet's nurse and Friar Laurence. Their young love is relished, amplified, and defended. Both lovers make it clear that they will commit suicide if they cannot be together.

Shakespeare foreshadows their dual deaths, fueled by a long-standing family feud between the Capulets and the Montagues. Romeo proclaims, "Come, death, and welcome. Juliet wills it so." Juliet has a vision of Romeo, "As one dead in the bottom of a tomb."[30] Angered after she discovers that her father wants her to marry Paris, Juliet goes to Friar Laurence and threatens to kill herself if she is so forced. Simultaneously, Romeo defends his love for Juliet and professes his willingness to die if he must live without her, declaring, "Then love-devouring death do what he dare, It is enough I may but call her mine."[30]

The idea of dying if they cannot be together is shared, relished, and amplified throughout the two lovers' interactions. Their spirited resolve becomes a decision that is ultimately binary and absolute. Eventually, Juliet is offered a solution by the friar. They concoct a plan in which she feigns death by drinking a sleeping potion as a ploy to be with Romeo. However, Romeo never gets word of the plan and thinks Juliet is truly dead. He buys poison, goes to the Capulet tomb, kills Paris, and then kills himself with the poison. Horrified by the quick turn of events, Juliet kisses Romeo in an attempt to get some of the poison from his lips. Finding that there is none left, she instead dies by stabbing herself with his dagger, proclaiming: "O happy dagger. This is thy sheath. There rust and let me die."[30] She relishes the penetrative and ecstatic union in death and the opportunity to die, for love.

Such passion is not limited to fiction. It periodically surfaces in actuality in the modern world. In 2012, in Mumbai, India, two lovers who were unable to convince their families to let them marry jumped in front of the Punjab Express train between Khadawali and Titwala stations. Witnesses said they hugged before the train hit them.[31]

Similarly, in 2013, in Queens, New York, two lovers pressured to end their relationship jumped in front of a Long Island Railroad commuter train. A lengthy suicide note stated that they were headed to "paradise" together. They left behind a two-year-old daughter.[32]

Were the actions of these couples validated in some way by Shakespeare's romanticizing of love and death? Did they see themselves as Romeo and Juliet? That's hard to say. But the existence of the overvalued "collective identity" reflected in the play certainly resonates with lovers who, forbidden to be together in life, choose to do so in a spirited death.

Epilogue

Extreme Overvalued Beliefs and Criminal Law

The scenarios documented throughout this book all lead to a relatively simple question—are fixed, false, idiosyncratic beliefs different from shared subcultural beliefs? Utilizing concise definitions of fixations may hold the key to better understanding the motives behind targeted attacks. The next logical step is to think about causation, as Swiss-German psychiatrist Karl Jaspers pondered in the last century. Paul McHugh, professor emeritus at Johns Hopkins notes:[1]

> Jaspers knew that some mental disorders derive from brain diseases, and therefore psychiatrists should be close allies with neurologists. But he also knew that mental distress could emerge as consequences of some conflict between an individual's wishes and actual life circumstances, so psychiatrists should naturally share interests with students in the social and cultural disciplines.[1(p vii)]

This concept is foundational to understanding mass shootings and targeted attacks because the issue of the brain and its function (mind) continue to vex the field of psychiatry. The risk for psychiatric disorders is multifactorial and influenced by genetic background, early adverse experiences, and personality factors. Ken Weiss, a professor and forensic psychiatrist at the University of Pennsylvania, notes:

> Static anatomy is insufficient, and attempts at isolating it from other dynamics (genetic, epigenetic, and environmental, for example) have not played well in legal settings. The meme that brains are responsible for crimes must be resisted. Neuroimaging techniques themselves, such as magnetic resonance imaging, have now been called into question.[2(p37)]

Without actionable biomarkers for diagnosing mental illnesses, where can we go next? Does the concept of extreme overvalued belief (EOB) help matters in the pursuit of justice? Establishing the *mens rea* of an offender is usually necessary to prove guilt in a criminal trial. Prosecutors must prove beyond reasonable doubt that the defendant committed the offense with a culpable state of mind.[2,3] Justice Oliver Wendell Holmes, Jr., famously illustrated the concept of intent when he said, "even a dog knows the difference between being stumbled over and being kicked.[3(p241)]

INSANITY

Uncertainties about the human mind loom large when it comes to the insanity defense. English and U.S. law developed the insanity defense to relieve the accused of legal responsibility when his or her thinking and behavior are so impaired at the time of the crime as a result of mental illness that the defendant meets that jurisdiction's legal definition of insanity. Legal definitions of insanity vary, and some states do not even recognize the insanity defense. The fact that a defendant committed a crime because of a delusional belief is a common basis for an insanity defense.[4] In 2020 the U.S. Supreme Court ruled in *Kahler v. Kansas* that the due process clause does not require states to offer an insanity defense.[5,6]

In U.S. federal and many state jurisdictions, the burden of proof shifts to the defendant to prove the defense of insanity by clear and convincing evidence. If the defense utilizes the definition of delusion as a basis for a severe mental disorder, there is no counter-balancing definition for a jury to consider when it comes to heinous violent acts. Presumptive evidence of delusions can be difficult for the prosecution to overcome.[5] Carl Wernicke, understanding such limits of psychiatric definitions, believed that crimes motivated by overvalued ideas should not be exculpatory for criminal charges. He argued that by misidentifying motives as delusions, anyone could argue that a defendant is insane after the commission of a crime.[7,8] Therefore, individuals with EOBs (without other serious psychopathology) are unlikely to cross the legal threshold of insanity because they are not due to a severe mental disease or defect.

A point which has been raised by UCLA professor Joseph Pierre is whether EOB is a retributivist concept. He believes it could introduce prosecutorial bias to thwart defense strategies attempting to establish connections between criminal behavior and less than optimal mental health.[9] However, it must be pointed out that defendants with delusions (e.g., from schizophrenia) also could benefit from concise definitions during an insanity trial.[5] An expert's opinion on the ultimate issue of whether a belief is a delusion or not should not usurp the province of the jury. The jury is the trier of fact and should be assumed to possess the ability to determine whether an individual's behaviors arise from delusions or EOBs. As an illustration, the jury in the case of John Hinckley, Jr., could have been instructed to consider whether he had a spirited, intense emotional commitment to pursuing actress Jodi Foster, or whether he held fixed and false idiosyncratic beliefs (delusions) due to schizophrenia.[7,10]

In Hinckley's trial, the jury was shown letters that he had written to Foster in which he stated that he was going to "get Reagan" for her—leaving no clear method for examiners to show that Hinckley was not delusional and may instead have had an EOB.[7] A similar consideration could be given to Norwegian terrorist Anders Breivik's spirited beliefs (e.g., being a "Knight Templar").[8] Application of concise definitions allows juries a more calibrated way to consider cases in which odd, bizarre, or extreme beliefs are present.[7,8]

MITIGATING OR AGGRAVATING FACTOR

Finally, with regard to sentencing, violence motivated by EOBs could be a mitigating or aggravating factor. For example, some individuals might be vulnerable to developing EOBs (like the overvalued ideas seen in anorexia nervosa). This susceptibility may be due to underlying vulnerabilities in emotion, cognition, and motivation—known problems that exist in some mood disorders, developmental disorders, low intellectual functioning, brain injury, drug and alcohol use, and so on.[11] In the case of Nikolas Cruz (the school shooter in Parkland, Florida) the jury weighed controversial evidence that he had features of fetal alcohol syndrome. He was ultimately sentenced to life imprisonment instead of the death penalty.[12] There was little discussion regarding motives other than categorical DSM-5 diagnoses in his case.

In contrast, evidence of such factors could alternatively be used as an aggravating circumstance in cases where the EOB was present in an otherwise higher functioning adult. As an example, former U.S. Army Major and psychiatrist Nidal Malik Hassan (the Fort Hood shooter) was sentenced to death for his spirited Jihadist attack that killed 13 and injured 30. Similarly, cult leader Charles Manson (convicted of first-degree and conspiracy to commit murder), Anders Breivik (Norwegian terrorist), Osama bin Laden and Ayman al-Zawahiri (Al-Qaeda leaders) might be viewed thorough a more punitive lens for spreading EOBs to their respective followers.[13]

PREVENTION OF TARGETED ATTACKS

The next question that should be addressed is: Can EOBs be prevented or treated? There have been innovative psychotherapeutic and behavioral attempts to alter or modulate overvalued beliefs, including counterbalancing efforts and purposeful cognitive dissonance approaches, which may be promising for future development in counterterrorism.[13-16]

One approach used to prevent eating disorders in adolescent girls is an intervention known as the "Body Project." It is based on the social psychological principle of cognitive dissonance: the contemporaneous experience of conflicting attitudes, beliefs, or behaviors in a person. The main intervention, led by psychologist Eric Stice, involves encouraging participants to take an active stance by arguing against the culturally mandated thin ideal.[15] Participants experience cognitive dissonance and actually shift their belief systems to align with a healthier anti-thin ideal stance. The Body Project has been demonstrably successful in numerous high schools and over 140 college campuses, and with over 3.5 million girls and young women in 25 countries. This project revealed an incredible 60% reduction in the number of expected cases of eating disorders that would have theoretically emerged without this cognitive-based intervention. Utilizing a train-the-trainer approach, while protecting First Amendment rights, the Body Project's concept of cognitive dissonance could be harnessed as a valuable template for countering EOBs.[13,17] The material in Chapter 9 may also be of importance in developing cognitive dissonance tools. We know that a priori knowledge and moral schema development are required for a person to progress toward violence:

> Moral schema → emotions such as anger, humiliation, contempt, and disgust → extreme overvalued beliefs → pathway to future attack

Intervening at early stages, such as utilizing cognitive dissonance involving moral schemas, could be readily developed into primary prevention ("cognitive inoculation") strategies. Similar to the Body Project, the participant would be better equipped to resist moral schemas and progression to an EOB. Education regarding internet cognitive isoforms could provide conscious awareness that cognitive illusions, like movement in cartoon animation, become a potent recipe for the development, sustenance, and spread of online EOBs.

Meanwhile, the "Violence Project," co-founded by psychologist Jillian Peterson and sociologist James Densley, is taking a holistic approach to mass-shooting prevention.[16] They offer solutions such as home visitation and family-preservation services, as well as reporting practices, batterer treatment programs, record keeping, and collaborative law enforcement approaches; their consistent conclusions are drawn from impressive research data.

THREAT ASSESSMENT AND MANAGEMENT

The detection of EOBs in the community is a far different challenge than any retrospective analysis in forensics. However, detection may be possible through screening questions centering on the following themes. Does an individual:[13]

- Relish extreme beliefs? (enjoys discussion of radical views)
- Possess extreme beliefs that dominate his or her mind? (won't easily change the subject)
- Bring up EOB in professional, social, school, or intimate settings when judged grossly inappropriate by others, resulting in anger, rejection, or confusion by others?
- Exhibit extreme beliefs that are growing more refined and resistant to challenge? (cannot see it from another perspective.)
- Use the internet to look up radical views that align with their own?
- Know or view videos of charismatic figures that hold similar extreme views?

- Quickly dismiss, argue, or avoid engagement with others who do not hold the beliefs?
- Frequently fill in missing and logical cognitive gaps to create a grand, albeit distorted, narrative?
- Display a confirmatory bias which is clearly evident and pervasive in the refusal to let contrary facts challenge or alter his beliefs?
- Exhibit beliefs that others feel are accompanied by a strong and constant emotional push or press in the subject?
- Have plans, or is mobilizing and identifying with violence, to express his EOB?
- Exhibit a different cognitive affective driver for his fixation (e.g., delusion and obsession) that has been ruled out?[13(p184)]

COUNTERING ONLINE BINARY BIAS

Since the brain is hardwired for binary bias (see Chapter 11), attention should be paid to the way consumers interact with social media. The current system provides and encourages the use of public feedback (emojis, likes, hearts, thumbs up/down) to respond to social media posts. These binary responses accelerate EOBs because the brain is hardwired to adopt what others believe—particularly concerning morally charged issues. As French psychologist Gustave Le Bon described in his 1895 work, *The Crowd*, the personality of an individual in a crowd is submerged, such that the collective crowd mind dominates (contagion) and is unanimous, emotional, and intellectually weak.[18] Nowhere is this observation more apparent than on social media, with its echo chamber and powerful distorting effects.[19]

Strategies to reduce Le Bon's *Crowd* effect are desperately needed—without dampening free speech. One way might be to change response options to social media posts. This could be done using Likert-type scales (similar to the internet movie database,[20] where movies are rated from 1 to 10). This could help reduce the contagion effect of messaging involving moral themes which are known to fuel feelings of anger, contempt, humiliation, and disgust in humans—all while protecting First Amendment rights.

Psychopathology does not come in neat categories of disorders described in psychiatric manuals. We have exposed an important flaw in the description of extreme or odd, rigidly held beliefs that the legal system should pay close attention to.[5] Recently the U.S. Supreme Court concluded that "defining the precise relationship between criminal culpability and mental illness involves examining the workings of the brain, the purposes of the criminal law, the ideas of free will and responsibility."[21(p24)] Indeed, the Court went on to state that the insanity defense "should be open to revision over time, as new medical knowledge emerges and as legal and moral norms evolve."[21(p24)] We have reached back over a century to provide a fresh approach to phenomenology in psychiatry and hope it sheds light on causal processes of criminal behavior.

REFERENCES

PREFACE

1. Kroll J, Pouncey C. The ethics of APA's Goldwater Rule. *Journal of the American Academy of Psychiatry and the Law.* 2016;44(2):226–35.
2. Martin-Joy J. Goldwater v. Ginzburg. *American Journal of Psychiatry.* 2015;172(8):729–30.
3. Appelbaum PS. Reflections on the Goldwater Rule. *The Journal of the American Academy of Psychiatry and the Law.* 2017;45(2):228–32.
4. Appel JM, Michels-Gualtieri A. Goldwater after Trump. *Cambridge Quarterly of Healthcare Ethics.* 2021;30(4):651–61.
5. Martin-Joy J. Interpreting the Goldwater Rule. *The Journal of the American Academy of Psychiatry and the Law.* 2017;45(2):233–40.

CHAPTER 1

1. Ledur J, Rabinowitz K, Galocha A. There have been over 300 mass shootings so far in 2022. *Washington Post.* June 2, 2022. https://www.washingtonpost.com/nation/2022/06/02/mass-shootings-in-2022/ (accessed August 22, 2022).
2. Rahman T, Resnick PJ, Harry B. Anders Breivik: Extreme beliefs mistaken for psychosis. *The Journal of the American Academy of Psychiatry and the Law.* 2016;4(1):28–35.
3. Macklin G, Bjørgo T. Breivik's long shadow? The impact of the July 22, 2011 attacks on the modus operandi of extreme-right lone actor terrorists. *Perspectives on Terrorism.* 2021;15(3):14–36.
4. Abbas T, Somoano I, Cook J, Frens I, Klein GR, McNeil-Willson R. The Buffalo attack: An analysis of the manifesto. *ICCT Journal.* 2022. https://icct.nl/publication/the-buffalo-attack-an-analysis-of-the-manifesto/ (accessed August 22, 2022).
5. Guldimann A, Meloy JR. Assessing the threat of lone-actor terrorism: The reliability and validity of the TRAP-18. *Forensische Psychiatrie, Psychologie, Kriminologie.* 2020;14(2):158–66.
6. Meloy JR, Gill P. The lone-actor terrorist and the TRAP-18. *Journal of Threat Assessment and Management.* 2016;3(1):37.
7. Jenkins J, Tandoc EC Jr. The power of the cover: Symbolic contests around the Boston bombing suspect's Rolling Stone cover. *Journalism.* 2017;18(3):281–97.

8. Burrows D. Investigative Committee on the Robb Elementary School (Uvalde) Shooting-Interim Report. 2022. https://policycommons.net/artifacts/2539952/documentcloud/3562381/ (accessed August 22, 2022).
9. Halverson JR, Goodall HL, Corman SR. *Master Narratives of Islamist Extremism*. New York: Palgrave Macmillan; 2011.
10. Rahman T, Hartz SM, Xiong W, Meloy JR, Janofsky J, Harry B, Resnick PJ. Extreme overvalued beliefs. *The Journal of the American Academy of Psychiatry and the Law*. 2020; 48(3):319–26.
11. Rahman T, Meloy JR, Bauer R. Extreme overvalued belief and the legacy of Carl Wernicke. *The Journal of the American Academy of Psychiatry and the Law* . 2019;47:180–87.
12. Oyebode F. *Sims' Symptoms in the Mind: An Introduction to Descriptive Psychopathology*. 4th edition. Philadelphia: Elsevier Health Sciences; 2008.
13. Gelder M, Gath D, Mayou R, Cowan P, eds. *Oxford Textbook of Psychiatry*. 3rd edition. New York: Oxford University Press; 1996.
14. Fish FJ. *An Outline of Psychiatry for Students and Practitioners*. 2nd edition. Bristol, UK: John Wright and Sons; 1968.
15. American Psychiatric Association. *Diagnostic and Statistical Manual of Mental Disorders*. 5th edition. Washington, DC: American Psychiatric Press; 2013.
16. McHugh PR. *The Mind Has Mountains: Reflections on Society and Psychiatry*. Baltimore, MD: Johns Hopkins University Press; 2006.
17. Zorumski C, Rubin E. *Psychiatry and Clinical Neuroscience: A Primer*. New York: Oxford University Press; 2011.
18. Freudenreich O. *Psychotic Disorders*. Boston: Springer International; 2020.
19. Wernicke C. Ueber fixe Ideen. *Deutsche Medicinische Wochenschrift* . 1892;25:2.
20. Wernicke C. *Grundriss der Psychiatriein Klinischen Vorlesungen* [Foundation of Psychiatry in Clinical Lectures]. Leipzig: Fischer & Wittig; 1900.
21. Miller R, Dennison JP, eds. *An Outline of Psychiatry in Clinical Lectures: The Lectures of Carl Wernicke*. New York: Springer; 2015.
22. Rahman T. Extreme overvalued beliefs: How violent extremist beliefs become "normalized." *Behavioral Sciences*. 2018;8(1):10.
23. Rahman T, Zheng L, Meloy JR. DSM-5 cultural and personality assessment of extreme overvalued beliefs. *Aggression and Violent Behavior*. 2021;60:101552.
24. Meloy JR, Habermeyer E, Guldimann A. The warning behaviors of Anders Breivik. *Journal of Threat Assessment and Management*. 2015;2:164–175.
25. Ghaemi SN. Nosologomania. DSM & Karl Jaspers' Critique of Kraepelin. *Philosophy, Ethics, and Humanities in Medicine*. 2009;4(1):1–8.
26. Reid Meloy J, Yakeley J. The violent true believer as a "lone wolf": Psychoanalytic perspectives on terrorism. *Behavioral Sciences & the Law*. 2014;32(3):347–65.
27. Gorski M. Karl Jaspers on delusion: Definition by genus and specific difference. *Philosophy, Psychiatry, & Psychology*. 2012;19(2):79–86.
28. Sims, Andrew. *Is Faith Delusion? Why Religion Is Good for Your Health*. London: Continuum; 2009.
29. Anderson M, McMillan N. 1,000 people have been charged for the Capitol riot. Here's where their cases stand. *NPR*. March 25, 2023. https://www.npr.org/2023/03/25/1165022885/1000-defendants-january-6-capitol-riot (accessed May 30, 2023).

30. Akiskal H. Diagnosis in psychiatry and the mental status examination. In: Winokur G, Clayton P, eds. *The Medical Basis of Psychiatry*. Philadelphia: W. B. Saunders; 1986:369–83.
31. Freudenreich O. *Psychotic Disorders: A Practical Guide*. Philadelphia: Lippincott Williams and Wilkins; 2007.
32. Meloy JR, Rahman T. *Extreme Overvalued Beliefs: Threat Assessment and Management*. Presentation at the 30th Annual Threat Assessment Conference, Anaheim CA, August 9, 2022.
33. American Psychiatric Association. *Diagnostic and Statistical Manual of Mental Disorders*. 5th edition, text revision. Washington, DC: American Psychiatric Press; 2022.

CHAPTER 2

1. Mullen PE, James DV, Meloy JR, Pathé MT, Farnham FR, Preston L, Darnley B, Berman J. The fixated and the pursuit of public figures. *The Journal of Forensic Psychiatry & Psychology*. 2009; 20(1):33–47.
2. Meloy JR. Empirical basis and forensic application of affective and predatory violence. *Australian & New Zealand Journal of Psychiatry*. 2006;40(6–7):539–47.
3. Monahan J, Steadman H. *Violence and Mental Disorder: Developments in Risk Assessment*. Chicago: University of Chicago Press; 1994.
4. Meloy JR, Rahman T. Cognitive-affective drivers of fixation in threat assessment. *Behavioral Sciences & the Law*. 2021;39(2):170–89.
5. James DV, Mullen PE, Meloy JR, Pathé MT, Farnham FR, Preston L, Darnley B. The role of mental disorder in attacks on European politicians 1990–2004. *Acta Psychiatrica Scandinavica*. 2007;116(5):334–44.
6. Burrows D. Texas House Investigative Committee on the Robb Elementary School (Uvalde) Shooting. Report. July 17, 2022. https://house.texas.gov/_media/pdf/committees/reports/87interim/Robb-Elementary-Investigative-Committee-Report.pdf (accessed May 23, 2023).
7. Rahman T, Resnick PJ, Harry B. Anders Breivik: Extreme beliefs mistaken for psychosis. *Journal of the American Academy of Psychiatry and the Law Online*. 2016;44(1):28–35.
8. Rahman T, Hartz SM, Xiong W, Meloy JR, Janofsky J, Harry B, Resnick PJ. Extreme overvalued beliefs. *The Journal of the American Academy of Psychiatry and the Law*. 2020;48(3):319–26.
9. American Psychiatric Association. *Diagnostic and Statistical Manual of Mental Disorders*. 5th edition. Washington, DC: American Psychiatric Press; 2013.
10. World Health Organization (WHO). The ICD-11 classification of mental and behavioural disorders. https://www.who.int/news/item/11-02-2022-icd-11-2022-release (accessed October 12, 2023).
11. Jaspers K. *Allgemeine psychopathologie: Ein Leitfaden fur Studierende, Arzte und Psychologen*. Berlin: Springer; 1913.
12. Rabins PV. Schizophrenia and psychotic states. In: Birren JE, Cohen GD, Sloane RB, Lebowitz BD, Deutchman DE, Wykle M, Hooyman NR, eds. *Handbook of Mental Health and Aging*. San Diego: Academic Press; 1992: 463–75.

13. Rahman T, Meloy JR, Bauer R. Extreme overvalued belief and the legacy of Carl Wernicke. *The Journal of the American Academy of Psychiatry and the Law.* 2019;47(2):180–87.
14. McHugh PR, Slavney PR. *The Perspectives of Psychiatry.* Baltimore, MD: Johns Hopkins University Press; 1998.
15. Rosen C, Grossman LS, Harrow M, Bonner-Jackson A, Faull R. Diagnostic and prognostic significance of Schneiderian first-rank symptoms: A 20-year longitudinal study of schizophrenia and bipolar disorder. *Comprehensive Psychiatry.* 2011;52(2):126–31.
16. Schneider K. *Clinical Psychopathology.* Translated by MW Hamilton. New York: Grune & Stratton; 1959.
17. Rahman T, Lauriello J. Schizophrenia: An overview. *Focus.* 2016;14(3):300–7.
18. Meloy JR, Habermeyer E, Guldimann A. The warning behaviors of Anders Breivik. *Journal of Threat Assessment and Management.* 2015;2(3–4):164.
19. Winokur G. Delusional disorder (paranoia). *Comprehensive Psychiatry.* 1977;18(6):511–21.
20. Oyebode F. *Sims' Symptoms in the Mind: An Introduction to Descriptive Psychopathology.* 4th edition. Philadelphia: Elsevier Health Sciences; 2008.
21. Veale D. Overvalued ideas: A conceptual analysis. *Behaviour Research and Therapy.* 2002;40(4):383–400.
22. Manschreck TC. Delusional disorder and shared psychotic disorder. In: Sadock BJ, Sadock VA, Ruiz P, eds. *Comprehensive Textbook of Psychiatry.* 7th edition. Baltimore, MD: Williams &Wilkins; 2000:1243–64.
23. Rahman T, Grellner KA, Harry B, Beck N, Lauriello J. Infanticide in a case of folie à deux. *American Journal of Psychiatry.* 2013; 170(10):1110–12.
24. Schneider RD. *The Lunatic and the Lords.* Toronto: Irwin Law; 2009.
25. Ciccone RJ. Daniel McNaughton: What did he do and why did he do it? Virtual lecture presented at: The American Academy of Psychiatry and the Law Expert Series; January 22, 2022.
26. Appelbaum PS, Gutheil TG. *Clinical Handbook of Psychiatry and the Law.* Philadelphia: Lippincott Williams & Wilkins; 2007.
27. Meloy JR, Lorraine S, Hoffmann J. *Stalking, Threatening, and Attacking Public Figures: A Psychological and Behavioral Analysis.* New York: Oxford University Press; 2008.
28. Resnick PJ. The Andrea Yates case: Insanity on trial. *Cleveland State Law Review.* 2007;55:147.
29. Resnick PJ. The Andrea Yates case: Insanity on trial, presented at University of New Mexico Department of Law; March 31, 2011.
30. Goodman WK, Price LH, Rasmussen SA, Mazure C, Fleischmann RL, Hill CL, Heninger GR, Charney DS. The Yale-Brown obsessive compulsive scale: I. Development, use, and reliability. *Archives of General Psychiatry.* 1989;46(11):1006–11.
31. Goodman WK, Price LH, Rasmussen SA, Mazure C, Delgado P, Heninger GR, Charney DS. The Yale-Brown obsessive compulsive scale: II. Validity. *Archives of General Psychiatry.* 1989;46(11):1012–16.
32. Rasmussen AR, Nordgaard J, Parnas J. Schizophrenia-spectrum psychopathology in obsessive–compulsive disorder: An empirical study. *European Archives of Psychiatry and Clinical Neuroscience.* 2020;270(8):993–1002.

33. Tolin DF, Abramowitz JS, Kozak MJ, Foa EB. Fixity of belief, perceptual aberration, and magical ideation in obsessive–compulsive disorder. *Journal of Anxiety Disorders*. 2001;15(6):501–10.
34. Booth BD, Friedman SH, Curry S, Ward H, Stewart SE. Obsessions of child murder: underrecognized manifestations of obsessive-compulsive disorder. *The Journal of the American Academy of Psychiatry and the Law Online*. 2014;42(1):66–74.
35. Wu H, Hariz M, Visser-Vandewalle V, Zrinzo L, Coenen VA, Sheth SA, Bervoets C, Naesström M, Blomstedt P, Coyne T, Hamani C. Deep brain stimulation for refractory obsessive-compulsive disorder (OCD): Emerging or established therapy? *Molecular Psychiatry*. 2021;26(1):60–65.
36. Thorsen AL, Hagland P, Radua J, Mataix-Cols D, Kvale G, Hansen B, van den Heuvel OA. Emotional processing in obsessive-compulsive disorder: A systematic review and meta-analysis of 25 functional neuroimaging studies. *Biological Psychiatry: Cognitive Neuroscience and Neuroimaging*. 2018;3(6):563–71.
37. Maier, HW. Über katathyme Wahnbildung und Paranoia. *Zeitschrift für die gesamte Neurologie und Psychiatrie*. 1912;(13):555–610.
38. Wertham, F. The catathymic crisis: A clinical entity. *Archives of Neurology and Psychiatry*. 1937;(37):974–77.
39. Meloy JR. *Violent Attachments*. Northvale: Aronson; 1992.
40. Blackman N, Weiss JM, Lamberti JW. The sudden murderer: III. Clues to preventive interaction. *Archives of General Psychiatry*. 1963;8(3):289–94.
41. Weiss JM, Lamberti JW, Blackman N. The sudden murderer: A comparative analysis. *AMA Archives of General Psychiatry*. 1960;2:669–78.
42. Schlesinger LB. *Sexual Murder: Catathymic and Compulsive Homicides*. New York: CRC Press; 2004.
43. Meloy JR. A catathymic infanticide. *Journal of Forensic Sciences*. 2010;55(5):1393–96.
44. Eagleman D. The brain on trial. *The Atlantic*. 2011:112–23.
45. Helmer WJ. The madman on the tower. *Texas Monthly*. 1986;14(8):169–71.
46. Jhanda S, Singla N, Grover S. Methylphenidate-induced obsessive-compulsive symptoms: A case report and review of literature. *Journal of Pediatric Neurosciences*. 2016;4:316.

CHAPTER 3

1. Dumas A. *Les trois mousquetaires* [The Three Musketeers]. Рипол Классик; London: Bruce and Wyld; 1846.
2. Warrick J. *Black Flags: The Rise of ISIS*. New York: Anchor; 2015.
3. Hempel AG, Meloy, JR, Richards TC. Offender and offense characteristics of a nonrandom sample of mass murderers. *Journal of the American Academy of Psychiatry and the Law*. 1999;27(2):213–25.
4. Langman P. Rampage school shooters: A typology. *Aggression and Violent Behavior*. 2009;14(1):79–86.
5. Meloy JR, Gill P. The lone-actor terrorist and the TRAP-18. *Journal of Threat Assessment and Management*. 2016;3(1):37–52.
6. Rahmani F, Hemmati A, Cohen SJ, Meloy JR. The interplay between antisocial and obsessive-compulsive personality characteristics in cult-like religious

groups: A psychodynamic decoding of the DSM-5. *International Journal of Applied Psychoanalytic Studies*. 2019;16(4):258–73.
7. Meloy JR, Hoffmann J, editors. *International Handbook of Threat Assessment*. 2nd Edition. New York: Oxford University Press; 2021.
8. Berger JM. *Extremism*. Cambridge, MA: MIT Press; 2018.
9. Gibson JW. *Warrior Dreams*. New York: Farrar, Straus & Giroux; 1994.
10. Meloy JR. Sexual desire, violent death, and the true believer. *Contemporary Psychoanalysis*. 2018;54:64–83.
11. Strozier C, Terman D, Jones J. *The Fundamentalist Mindset: Psychological Perspectives on Religion, Violence, and History*. New York: Oxford University Press; 2010.
12. Robles F. Dylann Roof photos and a manifesto are posted on website. *New York Times*. June 20, 2015. https://www.nytimes.com/2015/06/21/us/dylann-storm-roof-photos-website-charleston-church-shooting.html (accessed June 3, 2023).
13. Meloy JR, Fisher H. Some thoughts on the neurobiology of stalking. *Journal of Forensic Science*. 2005 November;50(6):JFS2004508-9.
14. Meloy JR. Unrequited love and the wish to kill: Diagnosis and treatment of borderline erotomania. *Bulletin of the Menninger Clinic*. 1989;53(6):477.
15. Rahman T. Extreme overvalued beliefs: How violent extremist beliefs become "normalized." *Behavioral Sciences*. 2018;8(1):10.
16. Rahman T, Meloy JR, Bauer R. Extreme overvalued belief and the legacy of Carl Wernicke. *The Journal of the American Academy of Psychiatry and the Law*. 2019;47(2):180–87.
17. Meloy JR, Habermeyer E, Guldimann A. The warning behaviors of Anders Breivik. *Journal of Threat Assessment and Management*. 2015;2(3–4):164.
18. Rahman T, Resnick PJ, Harry B. Anders Breivik: Extreme beliefs mistaken for psychosis. *The Journal of the American Academy of Psychiatry and the Law*. 2016;44(1):28–35.
19. Meloy JR, Mohandie K, Knoll JL, Hoffmann J. The concept of identification in threat assessment. *Behavioral Sciences & the Law*. 2015;33(2–3):213–37.
20. Cunningham MD. Differentiating delusional disorder from the radicalization of extreme beliefs: A 17-factor model. *Journal of Threat Assessment and Management*. 2018;5(3):137.
21. Acklin MW. Beyond the boundaries: Ethical issues in the practice of indirect personality assessment in non-health-service psychology. *Journal of Personality Assessment*. 2018;102(2):269–77.
22. Meloy JR. Indirect personality assessment of the violent true believer. *Journal of Personality Assessment*. 2004;82(2):138–46.
23. Meloy JR. *Psychological Tests and Report of Timothy McVeigh*. April 5, 1991. https://drreidmeloy.com/wp-content/uploads/2021/11/Unpublished_TimMcVeighPsychTesting.pdf (accessed May 31, 2023).
24. Toobin J. *Homegrown: Timothy McVeigh and the Rise of Right-Wing Extremism*. New York: Simon and Schuster; 2023.
25. Meloy JR, Rahman T. Cognitive-affective drivers of fixation in threat assessment. *Behavioral Sciences & the Law*. 2021;39(2):170–89.
26. Lehmann C. The enemy within. *Washington Post*. April 15, 2001. https://www.washingtonpost.com/archive/entertainment/books/2001/04/15/the-enemy-within/5ae9ddec-83b5-4cca-9701-a4217a68426b/ (accessed May 31, 2023).

27. McVeigh won't use insanity defense. *Spokesman Review*. November 17, 1995. https://www.spokesman.com/stories/1995/nov/17/mcveigh-wont-use-insanity-defense/ (accessed June 3, 2023).
28. Meloy JR, Genzman J. The clinical threat assessment of the lone-actor terrorist. *Psychiatric Clinics*. 2016;39(4):649–62.
29. U.S. Senate Committee on Homeland Security and Governmental Affairs. A ticking time bomb: Counterterrorism lessons from the U.S. Government's failure to prevent the Fort Hood attack. 2011. http://www.hsgac.senate.gov (accessed August 22, 2022).
30. Full Report of Sanity Board, US vs. Nidal Hasan . January 13, 2011. https://archive.nytimes.com/www.nytimes.com/interactive/2013/08/13/us/hasan-documents.html (accessed August 22, 2022).
31. Poppe, K. Nidal Hasan: A case study in lone-actor terrorism. Washington, DC: George Washington University: Program on Extremism. October 2018. https://extremism.gwu.edu/sites/g/files/zaxdzs2191/f/Nidal%20Hasan.pdf (accessed August 22, 2022).
32. *United States v. Cesar Altieri Sayoc*, 18 Cr 820 (JSR). https://www.courthousenews.com/wp-content/uploads/2019/07/Sayoc-Sentencing-Submission.pdf (accessed August 22, 2022).
33. Date J. Mail bomber Cesar Sayoc obsessed with Trump, Fox News, chilling new court filings show. *ABC News*. July 23, 2019. https://abcnews.go.com/US/mail-bomber-cesar-sayoc-obsessed-trump-fox-news/story?id=64500598 (accessed June 3, 2023).
34. Zapotosky M, Gowen A, Horwitz S, Wootson CR Jr. Who is Cesar Sayoc? What we know about the suspected mail bomber arrested in Florida. *Washington Post*. October 26, 2018. https://www.washingtonpost.com/nation/2018/10/26/who-is-cesar-altieri-sayoc-what-we-know-about-suspected-mail-bomber-arrested-florida/ (accessed June 3, 2023).
35. Meloy JR. *Violent Attachments*. Northvale: Aronson; 1992.
36. Freudenreich O. *Psychotic Disorders: A Practical Guide*. Philadelphia: Lippincott Williams and Wilkins; 2007.

CHAPTER 4

1. Meloy JR, Hoffmann J, eds. *International Handbook of Threat Assessment*. 2nd edition. New York: Oxford University Press; 2021.
2. Meloy JR. The operational development and empirical testing of the Terrorist Radicalization Assessment Protocol (TRAP–18). *Journal of Personality Assessment*. 2018;100(5):483–92.
3. Meloy JR, Gill P. The lone-actor terrorist and the TRAP-18. *Journal of Threat Assessment and Management*. 2016;3(1):37.
4. Meloy JR. The operational development and empirical testing of the Terrorist Radicalization Assessment Protocol (TRAP–18). *Journal of Personality Assessment*. 2018;100(5):483–92.
5. James DV, Mullen PE, Pathé MT, Meloy JR, Farnham FR, Preston L, Darnley B. Attacks on the British royal family: The role of psychotic illness. *The Journal of the American Academy of Psychiatry and the Law*. 2008;36(1):59–67.

6. Dietz PE, Martell DA. Mentally disordered offenders in pursuit of celebrities and politicians. Inter-university Consortium for Political and Social Research; U.S. Department of Justice. 1989. https://www.ojp.gov/ncjrs/virtual-library/abstracts/mentally-disordered-offenders-pursuit-celebrities-and-politicians (accessed June 4, 2023).
7. Reid JR, Hoffmann J, Guldimann A, James D. The role of warning behaviors in threat assessment: An exploration and suggested typology. *Behavioral Sciences & the Law*. 2012;30(3): 256–79.
8. Douglas KS, Skeem JL. Violence risk assessment: Getting specific about being dynamic. *Psychology, Public Policy, and Law*. 2005;11(3):347.
9. Guldimann A, Meloy JR. Assessing the threat of lone-actor terrorism: The reliability and validity of the TRAP-18. *Forensische Psychiatrie, Psychologie, Kriminologie*. 2020;14(2):158–66.
10. Meloy JR, Hoffmann J, Roshdi K, Guldimann A. Some warning behaviors discriminate between school shooters and other students of concern. *Journal of Threat Assessment and Management*. 2014;1(3):203.
11. Ilic A, Frei A. Mass murder and consecutive suicide in Switzerland: A comparative analysis. *Journal of Threat Assessment and Management*. 2019;6(1):23.
12. Meloy JR, Rahman T. Cognitive-affective drivers of fixation in threat assessment. *Behavioral Sciences & the Law*. 2021;39(2):170–89.
13. Meloy JR, O'Toole ME. The concept of leakage in threat assessment. *Behavioral Sciences & the Law*. 2011;29(4):513–27.
14. Challacombe DJ, Lucas PA. Postdicting violence with sovereign citizen actors: An exploratory test of the TRAP-18. *Journal of Threat Assessment and Management*. 2019;6(1):51.
15. García-Andrade RF, Rendón-Luna BS, Prieto BR, Martínez VV, de Meneses EM, Rodríguez EF. Forensic-psychiatric assessment of the risk of terrorist radicalisation in the mentally ill patient. *Spanish Journal of Legal Medicine*. 2019;45(2):59–66.
16. Lloyd M, Dean C. The development of structured guidelines for assessing risk in extremist offenders. *Journal of Threat Assessment and Management*. 2015;2(1):40.
17. Pressman DE. Risk Assessment Decisions for Violent Political Extremism. 2009. https://hope-radproject.org/wp-content/uploads/2021/12/Pressman-2009-Risk-assessment-decisions-for-violent-political-extremism.pdf (accessed June 3, 2023).
18. Douglas KS, Hart SD, Webster CD, Belfrage H, Eaves D. HCR–V3 Historical Clinical Risk Management (version 3): Professional guidelines for evaluating risk for violence. Mental Health, Law and Policy Institute, Simon Fraser University, Burnaby; 2013.
19. Hart SD, Hare RD, Harpur TJ. The Psychopathy Checklist—Revised (PCL–R): An overview for researchers and clinicians. *Advances in Psychological Assessment*. 1992:8:103–30.
20. Beyli-Helmy M, Habermeyer E, Guldimann A. Was kann die Forensische Psychologie und Psychiatrie im Bedrohungsmanagement beitragen? Erkenntnisse aus der interdisziplinären Zusammenarbeit im Kanton Zürich. *Rechtspsychologie—RPsych*. 2020;6(3):357–70.
21. Rahman T, Hartz SM, Xiong W, Meloy JR, Janofsky J, Harry B, Resnick PJ. Extreme overvalued beliefs. *The Journal of the American Academy of Psychiatry and the Law*. 2020;48(3):319–26.

22. Rahman T, Lauriello J. Schizophrenia: An overview. *Focus*. 2016 Jul;14(3):300–7.
23. Meloy JR. A catathymic infanticide. *Journal of Forensic Sciences*. 2010;55(5): 1393–96.
24. Braun DL, Sunday SR, Halmi KA. Psychiatric comorbidity in patients with eating disorders. *Psychological Medicine*. 1994;24(4):859–67.
25. Corner E, Gill P. A false dichotomy? Mental illness and lone-actor terrorism. *Law and Human Behavior*. 2015;39(1):23.
26. Kupper J, Cotti P, Meloy JR. The Hanau terror attack: Unraveling the dynamics of mental disorder and extremist beliefs. *Journal of Threat Assessment and Management*. 2023. https://psycnet.apa.org/doi/10.1037/tam0000201.

CHAPTER 5

1. Gull W. Anorexia nervosa. *The Lancet*. 1888:131(3368):516–17.
2. Shapiro F. You can quote them, you can't be too rich or too thin. *Yale Alumni Magazine*. January–February 2008. https://yalealumnimagazine.org/articles/1966-you-can-quote-them (accessed September 13, 2022).
3. Preti A, Rocchi MB, Sisti D, Camboni MV, Miotto P. A comprehensive meta-analysis of the risk of suicide in eating disorders. *Acta Psychiatrica Scandinavica*. 2011;124(1):6–17.
4. Shih PA, Woodside DB. Contemporary views on the genetics of anorexia nervosa. *European Neuropsychopharmacology*. 2016;26 (4):663–73.
5. Hay PJ, Sachdev P. Brain dysfunction in anorexia nervosa: Cause or consequence of under-nutrition? *Current Opinion in Psychiatry*. 2011;24(3):251–56.
6. Oyebode F. *Sims' Symptoms in the Mind: An Introduction to Descriptive Psychopathology*. 4th edition. Philadelphia: Elsevier Health Sciences; 2008.
7. Rahman T, Hartz SM, Xiong W, Meloy JR, Janofsky J, Harry B, Resnick PJ. Extreme overvalued beliefs. *The Journal of the American Academy of Psychiatry and the Law*. 2020;48 (3):319–26.
8. McHugh PR. *The Mind Has Mountains: Reflections on Society and Psychiatry*. Baltimore, MD: Johns Hopkins University Press; 2006.
9. Pierson B. Two new lawsuits claim Meta's Instagram caused eating disorders. *Reuters*. July 25, 2022. https://www.reuters.com/legal/litigation/two-new-lawsuits-claim-metas-instagram-caused-eating-disorders-2022-07-25/ (accessed June 1, 2023).
10. Wilson JL, Peebles R, Hardy KK, Litt IF. Surfing for thinness: A pilot study of pro–eating disorder web site usage in adolescents with eating disorders. *Pediatrics*. 2006;118(6):e1635–43.
11. Zorumski C, Rubin E. *Psychiatry and Clinical Neuroscience: A Primer*. New York: Oxford University Press; 2011.
12. Meloy JR, Rahman T. Cognitive-affective drivers of fixation in threat assessment. *Behavioral Sciences & the Law*. 2021;39(2):170–89.
13. American Psychiatric Association. *Diagnostic and Statistical Manual of Mental Disorders*. 5th edition. Arlington, VA: American Psychiatric Press; 2013.
14. Phillips KA. Suicidality in body dysmorphic disorder. *Primary Psychiatry*. 2007;14(12):58.
15. Parker R. Body hatred. *British Journal of Psychotherapy*. 2003;19(4):447–64.

16. Phillips KA. *The Broken Mirror: Understanding and Treating Body Dysmorphic Disorder*. New York: Oxford University Press; 2005.
17. Jaspers K. *General Psychopathology*. Translated from the German 7th edition (1959) by J Hoenig and M Hamilton. Chicago: University of Chicago Press; 1963.
18. White S. Work Trauma Service, Inc. https://www.wtsglobal.com/ (accessed September 14, 2022).
19. Mullen PE, Lester G. Vexatious litigants and unusually persistent complainants and petitioners: From querulous paranoia to querulous behaviour. *Behavioral Sciences & the Law*. 2006;24(3):333–49.
20. Kraepelin E. *Clinical Psychiatry: A Text-Book for Students and Physicians*, Volume 2: *Clinical Psychiatry*. Translated by S Ayed, edited by JM Quen, MD. Canton: Watson; 1989.
21. Lester G, Wilson FB, Griffin L, Mullen PE. Unusually persistent complainants. *The British Journal of Psychiatry*. 2004; 184(4):352–56.
22. Meyer v. Merjanian, 4:21-00202-CV-RK (W.D. Mo.), document 30, filed August 17, 2021, page 3.
23. Mullen PE, Lester G. Vexatious litigants and unusually persistent complainants and petitioners: From querulous paranoia to querulous behaviour. *Behavioral Sciences & the Law*. 2006;24(3):333–49.
24. Mullen PE. Querulous behaviour: Vexatious litigation, abnormally persistent complaining and petitioning. In: Gelder MG, Andreasen NC, Lopez-Ibor JJ, Geddes JR, eds. *New Oxford Textbook of Psychiatry*, Volume 2. Oxford: Oxford University Press; 2009:1977–80.
25. Lester G, Wilson FB, Griffin L, Mullen PE. Unusually persistent complainants. *The British Journal of Psychiatry*. 2004;184(4):352–56.
26. Harris D. Deadly Arkansas shooting by "Sovereigns" Jerry and Joe Kane who shun U.S. law. *ABC News*, July 1, 2010. https://abcnews.go.com/WN/deadly-arkansas-shooting-sovereign-citizens-jerry-kane-joseph/story?id=11065285 (accessed September 14, 2022).
27. Sarteschi CM. Sovereign Citizens: A narrative review with implications of violence towards law enforcement. *Aggression and Violent Behavior*. 2021;60:101509.
28. Edge Staff. What you don't know about Sovereign Citizens can hurt you. American Military University. September 23, 2019. https://amuedge.com/what-you-dont-know-about-sovereign-citizens-can-hurt-you/ (accessed September 14, 2022).
29. Southern Poverty Law Center. Sovereign Citizens Movement. https://www.splcenter.org/fighting-hate/extremist-files/ideology/sovereign-citizens-movement (accessed September 14, 2022).
30. Parker GF. Competence to stand trial evaluations of Sovereign Citizens: A case series and primer of odd political and legal beliefs. *The Journal of the American Academy of Psychiatry and the Law*. 2014;42(3):338–49.
31. Schellhammer M. Attorney for McKean County woman held for Jan. 6 seeks release. *Olean Times Herald*. July 6, 2022. https://www.oleantimesherald.com/news/attorney-for-mckean-county-woman-held-for-jan-6-seeks-release/article_848575e2-f989-5782-a44e-15db4a603e88.html (accessed September 14, 2022).
32. Messerly M. Gunman who opened fire from Mandalay Bay sued the Cosmopolitan for a slip and fall years earlier. *The Nevada Independent*. https://thenevadaindepend

References

33. Goudie C. Chicago Lollapalooza was top "indicator of intent" for Las Vegas shooter. *ABC 7 Chicago Eyewitness News.* https://abc7chicago.com/lollapalooza-2018-chicago-2017-stephen-paddock/3878519/ (accessed September 14, 2022).
34. Pearce M, Kaleem J, Etehad M. In Las Vegas, the casino is always watching—and yet it missed Stephen Paddock. *Los Angeles Times.* October 12, 2017. https://www.latimes.com/nation/la-na-vegas-shooting-casino-security-20171012-story.html (accessed September 14, 2022).
35. Kovaleski SF, Maker M. Gunman in 2017 Las Vegas shooting was angry at casinos, new FBI files show. *New York Times.* March 30, 2023. https://www.nytimes.com/2023/03/30/us/las-vegas-shooting-gunman.html (accessed June 1, 2023).
36. Fink S. Las Vegas Gunman's brain exam only deepens mystery of his actions. *New York Times.* February 9, 2018. https://www.nytimes.com/2018/02/09/us/las-vegas-attack-paddock-brain-autopsy.html (accessed June 11, 2024).

CHAPTER 6

1. Swift A. Majority in U.S. still believe JFK killed in a conspiracy. *Gallup News.* November 15, 2013. https://news.gallup.com/poll/165893/majority-believe-jfk-killed-conspiracy.aspx (accessed June 1, 2023).
2. American Psychiatric Association. *Diagnostic and Statistical Manual of Mental Disorders.* 5th edition. Arlington, VA: American Psychiatric Press; 2013.
3. Abrahamsen D. A study of Lee Harvey Oswald: Psychological capability of murder. *Bulletin of the New York Academy of Medicine.* 1967;43(10):887.
4. Meloy JR, Rahman T. Cognitive-affective drivers of fixation in threat assessment. *Behavioral Sciences & the Law.* 2021;39(2):170–89.
5. Rahman T, Hartz SM, Xiong W, Meloy JR, Janofsky J, Harry B, Resnick PJ. Extreme overvalued beliefs. *The Journal of the American Academy of Psychiatry and the Law.* 2020;48 (3):319–26.
6. Meloy JR. *Terrorist Radicalization Assessment Protocol-18 Users' Manual 1.0.* Toronto: Multi-health Systems; 2017.
7. Meloy JR, Hoffmann J. *International Handbook of Threat Assessment.* 2nd edition. New York: Oxford University Press; 2021.
8. United States Commission on the Assassination of President John F. Kennedy, United States. Warren Commission. *Report of the President's Commission on the Assassination of President John F. Kennedy.* Washington, DC: US Government Printing Office; 1964. https://www.archives.gov/research/jfk/warren-commission-report.
9. Bugliosi V. *Reclaiming History: The Assassination of President John F. Kennedy.* New York: W. W. Norton; 2007.
10. Posner G. *Case Closed: Lee Harvey Oswald and the Assassination of JFK.* New York: Bantam Doubleday Dell Publishing Group; 1994.
11. Author correspondence with author Gerald Posner. August 24, 2021.
12. Miller M. Bob Dylan drops new song about JFK assassination, his first original release in 8 years. *Entertainment Weekly.* March 27, 2020. https://ew.com/music/bob-dylan-new-song-murder-most-foul-jfk-assassination/ (accessed June 1, 2023).

13. Chebrolu E. The racial lens of Dylann Roof: Racial anxiety and white nationalist rhetoric on new media. *Review of Communication*. 2020;20(1):47–68.
14. Rahman T, Zheng L, Meloy JR. DSM-5 cultural and personality assessment of extreme overvalued beliefs. *Aggression and Violent Behavior*. 2021;60:101552.
15. Mailer N. *Oswald's Tale: An American Mystery*. New York: Random House; 2007.
16. DeNooyer R, Tiffany S. Cold Case JFK. *Nova Episode*. Aired November 13, 2013.
17. History.com editors. An ex-Marine goes on a killing spree at the University of Texas. *A&E Television Networks*. https://www.history.com/this-day-in-history/an-ex-marine-goes-on-a-killing-spree-at-the-university-of-texas.
18. Rahman T, Meloy JR, Bauer R. Extreme overvalued belief and the legacy of Carl Wernicke. *The Journal of the American Academy of Psychiatry and the Law*. 2019:47(2):180–87.
19. Rahman T, Resnick PJ, Harry B. Anders Breivik: Extreme beliefs mistaken for psychosis. *The Journal of the American Academy of Psychiatry and the Law*. 2016;44(1):28–35.
20. Turchie TD, Puckett KM. *Hunting the American Terrorist: The FBI's War on Homegrown Terror*. Palisades, NJ: History Publishing; 2007.
21. Meloy JR. Indirect personality assessment of the violent true believer. *Journal of Personality Assessment*. 2004; 82(2):138–46.
22. Meloy RJ. *Violent Attachments*. Northvale, NJ: Aronson; 1998.
23. Sweeney A, Sobol R, McCoppin, R, Sheridan, J. Highland Park shooting: Man arrested apparently posted series of videos; investigators turn to source of rifle. *Chicago Tribune*. July 4, 2022. https://www.chicagotribune.com/news/breaking/ct-highland-park-shooting-gun-20220705-dltcauygmzfl7lyz5y5fvtfcte-story.html (accessed June 1, 2023).
24. Rothmann S, Coetzer EP. The big five personality dimensions and job performance. *SA Journal of Industrial Psychology*. 2003;29(1):68–74.
25. Freedman AM, Kaplan HI. *Comprehensive Texook of Psychiatry*. Baltimore, MD: The Williams and Wilkins Company; 1967.

CHAPTER 7

1. Froese P. *On Purpose: How We Create the Meaning of Life*. New York: Oxford University Press; 2016.
2. Silva JR, Greene-Colozzi EA. Fame-seeking mass shooters in America: Severity, characteristics, and media coverage. *Aggression and Violent Behavior*. 2019;48:24–35.
3. Connecticut State Police Sandy Hook Elementary School Shooting Report. https://cspsandyhookreport.ct.gov/ (accessed June 2, 2023).
4. Langman P. The enigma of Adam Lanza's mind and motivations for murder. *The Journal of Campus Behavioral Intervention*. 2015;3:1–11. http://maui.hawaii.edu/wp-content/uploads/sites/4/2018/09/JBIT-2015-Final.pdf#page=5 (accessed June 2, 2023).
5. Obama White House Archives. https://obamawhitehouse.archives.gov/blog/2012/12/14/president-obama-speaks-shooting-connecticut (accessed June 1, 2023).
6. Steinberg A. Can you erase the trauma from a place like Sandy Hook? *New York Times Magazine*. September 15, 2016. https://www.nytimes.com/2016/09/15/magaz

ine/can-you-erase-the-trauma-from-a-place-like-sandy-hook.html (accessed June 1, 2023).
7. Ortiz JL. Sandy Hook school shooter had "scorn for humanity," according to newly released documents. *USA Today.* December 9, 2018. https://www.usatoday.com/story/news/2018/12/09/sandy-hook-shooter-adam-lanza-had-scorn-humanity/2259413002/ (accessed June 1, 2023).
8. Bonvillian C. "Nothing but scorn for humanity": Documents show dark decline of Sandy Hook shooter Adam Lanza. *Cox Media Group, KIRO 7 News.* December 11, 2018. https://www.kiro7.com/news/trending-now/nothing-but-scorn-for-humanity-newly-released-writings-show-evolution-of-sandy-hook-shooter/886822030/ (accessed June 3, 2023).
9. Murray JL. Mass media reporting and enabling of mass shootings. *Cultural Studies, Critical Methodologies.* 2017;17(2):114–24.
10. Altimari D. Sandy Hook shooter Adam Lanza's spreadsheet detailing centuries of mass violence served as a road map to murder. *Hartford Courant.* December 9, 2018. https://www.courant.com/2018/12/09/sandy-hook-shooter-adam-lanzas-spreadsheet-detailing-centuries-of-mass-violence-served-as-a-road-map-to-murder/ (accessed June 3, 2023).
11. Veale D. Overvalued ideas: A conceptual analysis. *Behaviour Research and Therapy.* 2002;40(4):383–400.
12. Oyebode F: *Sims' Symptoms in the Mind: An Introduction to Descriptive Psychopathology.* 4th edition. Philadelphia: Elsevier Health Sciences; 2008.
13. Rylander M, Taylor G, Bennett S, Pierce C, Keniston A, Mehler PS. Evaluation of cognitive function in patients with severe anorexia nervosa before and after medical stabilization. *Journal of Eating Disorders.* 2020;8(1):1–10.
14. Carina Gillberg I, Råstam M, Wentz E, Gillberg C. Cognitive and executive functions in anorexia nervosa ten years after onset of eating disorder. *Journal of Clinical and Experimental Neuropsychology.* 2007;29(2):170–78.
15. Zorumski C, Rubin E. *Psychiatry and Clinical Neuroscience: A Primer.* New York: Oxford University Press; 2011.
16. Office of the Child Advocate. https://portal.ct.gov/-/media/OCA/SandyHook11212014pdf.pdf.
17. School Shooters.info. Langman Psychological Associates (compiled by Reed Coleman). https://schoolshooters.info/sites/default/files/lanza_posts_2.2.pdf (accessed June 2, 2023).
18. SchoolShooters.info. https://schoolshooters.info/sites/default/files/columbine_basement_tapes_1.0.pdf.
19. Internet Archive. Hitmen for Hire (Columbine Home Video). Langman Psychological Associates. https://archive.org/details/hitmanforhirecolumbinehomevideo (accessed June 1, 2023).
20. (Opinion) Our view: Death penalty repeal should apply to all. *The Bulletin.* April 2, 2013. https://www.norwichbulletin.com/story/opinion/editorials/2013/04/25/our-view-death-penalty-repeal/64938190007/
21. Sparks B, Zidenberg AM, Olver ME. One is the loneliest number: Involuntary celibacy (incel), mental health, and loneliness. *Current Psychology.* 2023;43(1):392–406.
22. Rahman T, Zheng L, Meloy JR. DSM-5 cultural and personality assessment of extreme overvalued beliefs. *Aggression and Violent Behavior.* 2021;60:101552.

CHAPTER 8

1. Le Bon G. *The Crowd: A Study of the Popular Mind*. 4th impression. London: T. Fisher Unwin; 1895.
2. Kupper J, Christensen TK, Wing D, Hurt M, Schumacher M, Meloy R. The contagion and copycat effect in transnational far-right terrorism. *Perspectives on Terrorism*. 2022;16 (4):4–26.
3. Turkle S. *Alone Together: Why We Expect More From Technology and Less From Each Other*. New York: Basic Books; 2011.
4. Andone D, Almasy S, Devine C. What we know about the Highland Park shooting suspect. *CNN*. July 5, 2022. https://www.cnn.com/2022/07/05/us/robert-e-crimo-highland-park-suspect/index.html.
5. Amarnath A. Argentino M-A. The Buffalo attack: The cumulative momentum of far right terror. *CTC Sentinel at West Point*. 2022;15(7):1–15.
6. Sapru D. Who is Buffalo shooter Payton Gendron of Conklin? Parents, charges against him, what exactly happened? *The Courier Daily*. May 17, 2022. https://www.thecourierdaily.com/who-buffalo-shooter-payton-gendron-parents-charges/24532/ (accessed June 1, 2023).
7. Rahman T, Zheng L, Meloy JR. DSM-5 cultural and personality assessment of extreme overvalued beliefs. *Aggression and Violent Behavior*. 2021;60:101552.
8. Meloy JR. *Terrorist Radicalization Assessment Protocol-18 Users' Manual 1.0*. Toronto: Multi-health Systems; 2017.
9. Pescara-Kovach L, Raleigh MJ. The contagion effect as it relates to public mass shootings and suicides. *The Journal of Campus Behavioral Intervention*. 2017;5:35–45.
10. White supremacists adopt new slogan: "You will not replace us." Anti-Defamation League. https://www.adl.org/blog/white-supremacists-adopt-new-slogan-you-will-not-replace-us (accessed June 3, 2023).
11. Bernstein L, Horwitz S, Holley P. Dylann Roof's racist manifesto: "I have no choice." *Washington Post*. June 20, 2015. https://www.washingtonpost.com/national/health-science/authorities-investigate-whether-racist-manifesto-was-written-by-sc-gunman/2015/06/20/f0bd3052-1762-11e5-9ddc-e3353542100c_story.html (accessed June 3, 2023).
12. Cinone D. Inside sick "Bowl Gang" that celebrates white supremacist church shooter Dylann Roof. news.com.au. https://www.news.com.au/lifestyle/real-life/true-stories/inside-sick-bowl-gang-that-celebrates-white-supremacist-church-shooter-dylann-roof/news-story/6a10cf86a33f2275bd7833835d9fc53 7.
13. Ware J. Testament to murder: The violent far-right's increasing use of terrorist manifestos. ICCT Policy Brief March 2020. https://www.jstor.org/stable/pdf/resrep23577.pdf (accessed June 3, 2023).
14. McCoy A, Garry A. Patrick Crusius Manifesto. American Counterterrorism Targeting & Resilience Institute. https://americanctri.org/wp-content/uploads/2020/12/ACTRI-Report-Edicts-Fatwas-and-Manifestos-McCoy-and-Garry.pdf (accessed June 3, 2023).
15. Martinez A. Federal trial in Walmart mass shooting at least a year away, even longer in state court. *El Paso Times*. August 22, 2020. https://www.elpasotimes.com/story/news/crime/2020/08/22/trial-el-paso-walmart-mass-shooting-least-year-away/5521472002/ (accessed June 3, 2023).

16. Department of Justice. Press release. Texas man pleads guilty to 90 federal hate crimes and firearms violations for August 2019 mass shooting at Walmart in El Paso, Texas. February 8, 2023. https://www.justice.gov/opa/pr/texas-man-pleads-guilty-90-federal-hate-crimes-and-firearms-violations-august-2019-mass (accessed June 2, 2023).
17. Coleman P. Targeting school shootings: using three warning signs—animal abuse, domestic violence, and conduct disorder—to help prevent massacres. *Widener Commonwealth Law Review.* 2023;32(1):65–133.
18. Spencer T. Parkland school shooter fixated with guns, dreamed of killing: Therapist letter. *NBC Miami 6.* https://www.nbcmiami.com/news/local/parkland-school-shooter-fixated-with-guns-dreamed-of-killing-therapist-letter/2843903/.
19. Brooks N, Shaw R. Fixated and grievance-fuelled persons: Considerations on the dangers of gaps, silos and disconnects. *Psychiatry, Psychology and Law.* 2022;29(6):854–70.
20. Foster-Frau S, Zakrzewski C, Nix N, Harwell D. Before massacre, Uvalde gunman frequently threatened teen girls online. *Washington Post.* May 28, 2022. https://www.washingtonpost.com/technology/2022/05/28/uvalde-texas-gunman-online-threats/.
21. Burrows D. Texas House Investigative Committee on the Robb Elementary School (Uvalde) Shooting: Report. July 17, 2022. https://house.texas.gov/_media/pdf/committees/reports/87interim/Robb-Elementary-Investigative-Committee-Report.pdf (accessed May 23, 2023).

CHAPTER 9

1. U.S. Department of Justice. Press Release. July 13, 2018. Grand jury indicts 12 Russian intelligence officers for hacking offenses related to the 2016 election. https://www.justice.gov/opa/pr/grand-jury-indicts-12-russian-intelligence-officers-hacking-offenses-related-2016-election (accessed June 3, 2023).
2. Shane S. The fake Americans Russia created to influence the election. *New York Times.* September 7, 2017:9.
3. Nacos B. *Mass-Mediated Terrorism: Mainstream and Digital Media in Terrorism and Counterterrorism.* Lanham, MD: Rowman & Littlefield; 2016.
4. U.S. Attorney's Office Southern District of California. Press Release. Santa Barbara man indicted in San Diego for killing his children in Mexico. September 8, 2021. https://www.justice.gov/usao-sdca/pr/santa-barbara-man-indicted-san-diego-killing-his-children-mexico.
5. Helling S. In letter from jail, Matthew Taylor Coleman admits "delusion in my own mind" before child murders. *People Magazine.* June 15, 2022. https://people.com/crime/matthew-taylor-coleman-letter-jail-admits-delusion/ (accessed June 4, 2023).
6. Kim J. U.S. Capitol rioter the "QAnon Shaman" is released early from federal prison. *NPR.* March 21, 2023. https://www.npr.org/2023/03/31/1167319814/qanon-shaman-jacob-chansley-capitol-riot-early-release-reentry (accessed June 4, 2023).
7. Concepcion S. "QAnon Shaman"' who stormed the Capitol on Jan. 6 files paperwork to run for Congress. *NBC News.* November 13, 2023. https://www.nbcnews.

com/politics/2024-election/qanon-shaman-stormed-capitol-jan-6-files-paperwork-run-congress-rcna124858
8. Wertheimer M. *Source Book of Gestalt Psychology*. New York: Harcourt, Brace; 1938.
9. Rock I, Palmer S. The legacy of Gestalt psychology. *Scientific American*. 1990;263(6):84–91.
10. Guberman S. On Gestalt theory principles. *Gestalt Theory*. 2015:37(1):25–44.
11. Peatfield N, Mueller N, Ruhnau P, Weisz N. Rubin-vase illusion perception is predicted by prestimulus activity and connectivity. *Journal of Vision*. 2015:15(12):429.
12. Furnham A, Boo HC. A literature review of the anchoring effect. *The Journal of Socio-Economics*. 2011:40(1):35–42.
13. Zorumski C, Rubin E. *Psychiatry and Clinical Neuroscience: A Primer*. New York: Oxford University Press; 2011.
14. King DB, Wertheimer M. *Max Wertheimer and Gestalt Theory*. New Brunswick, NJ: Transaction; 2005.
15. Beard RM. *An Outline of Piaget's Developmental Psychology*. Abingdon, UK: Routledge; 2013.
16. Loomba S, de Figueiredo A, Piatek SJ, de Graaf K, Larson HJ. Measuring the impact of COVID-19 vaccine misinformation on vaccination intent in the UK and USA. *Nature Human Behaviour*. 2021:5(3):337–48.
17. Jamieson KH, Cappella JN. *Echo Chamber: Rush Limbaugh and the Conservative Media Establishment*. New York: Oxford University Press; 2008.
18. Hathaway B. Online illusion: Unplugged, we really aren't that smart. *Yale News*. March 31, 2015. https://news.yale.edu/2015/03/31/online-illusion-unplugged-we-really-aren-t-smart (accessed June 4, 2023).
19. University College Press Office, Neuroscience News. Press Release. April 21, 2023. https://neurosciencenews.com/reality-illusion-brain-23075/ (accessed June 4, 2023).
20. Meloy JR, Pollard JW. Lone-actor terrorism and impulsivity. *Journal of Forensic Sciences*. 2017;62(6):1643–46.
21. Lim C, Van Alphen M, Freudenreich O. Becoming vaccine ambassadors: A new role for psychiatrists. *Current Psychiatry*. 2021;20(8):10–11.
22. *Schenck v. United States*, 249 U.S. 47 (1919).
23. Reuters News (Fact Check bulletin). BBC News broadcast claiming that nuclear war is imminent between Russia and NATO recirculates. January 24, 2022. https://www.reuters.com/article/factcheck-bbc-news-russia/fact-check-fake-bbc-news-broadcast-claiming-that-nuclear-war-is-imminent-between-russia-and-nato-recirculates-idUSL1N2U41K4 (accessed June 4, 2023).
24. Fisher M, Keil FC. The binary bias: A systematic distortion in the integration of information. *Psychological Science*. 2018;29(11):1846–58.
25. Asch SE. Effects of group pressure upon the modification and distortion of judgments. In: Guetzkknow H, ed. *Groups, Leadership, and Men*. Pittsburg: Carnegie Press; 1951:177–90.
26. Asch SE. *Social Psychology*. Englewood Cliffs, NJ: Prentice-Hall; 1952.
27. Sinclair-Chapman V. (De)constructing symbols: Charlottesville, the confederate flag, and a case for disrupting symbolic meaning. *Politics, Groups, and Identities*. 2018;6(2):316–23.

28. Meloy JR. *Terrorist Radicalization Assessment Protocol-18 Users' Manual 1.0*. Toronto: Multi-health Systems; 2017.
29. Matsumoto D, Hwang HC, Frank MG. Emotion and aggressive intergroup cognitions: The ANCODI hypothesis. *Aggressive Behavior*. 2017;43(1):93–107.
30. Donald Trump Jr compares Syrian refugees to Skittles. *BBC News*. September 20, 2016. https://www.bbc.com/news/election-us-2016-37416457 (accessed June 4, 2023).
31. Öhman A, Flykt A, Esteves F. Emotion drives attention: Detecting the snake in the grass. *Journal of Experimental Psychology*. 2001;130(3):466.
32. Snyder LL. *Hitler's Elite: Biographical Sketches of Nazis Who Shaped the Thrid Reich*. Worcester: David and Charles; 1989.
33. Larkin RW. Learning to Be a Rampage Shooter. In: Shapiro H, ed. *The Wiley Handbook on Violence in Education: Forms, Factors, and Preventions*. Hoboken: John Wiley and Sons; 2018.
34. Meloy JR. The theoretical frame. *Contemporary Psychoanalysis*. 2018:54(1):64–83.
35. Andrews E. 7 bizarre witch trial tests. *A&E Televisions Networks*. March 18, 2014. https://www.history.com/news/7-bizarre-witch-trial-tests.
36. Stepko B. The horrifying tests used in Salem to determine if a woman was a witch. *The Vintage News*. October 23, 2018. https://www.thevintagenews.com/2018/10/23/salem-witch/?edg-c=1 (accessed June 4, 2023).
37. Naila Mumtaz murder: Four family members jailed for life. *BBC News*. September 24, 2012. https://www.bbc.com/news/uk-england-birmingham-19699500.
38. Macy I. Man pleas guilty to murdering 4-year-old Jessica Mast. *KOLR News*. February 23, 2022. https://www.ozarksfirst.com/local-news/local-news-local-news/man-pleas-guilty-to-murdering-4-year-old-jessica-mast/.
39. McMahon B. Woman drowns during exorcism ceremony. *The Guardian*. November 12, 2007. https://www.theguardian.com/world/2007/nov/12/barbaramcmahon.
40. Rahman T, Zheng L, Meloy JR. DSM-5 cultural and personality assessment of extreme overvalued beliefs. *Aggression and Violent Behavior*. 2021; 60:101552.
41. McHugh PR, Slavney PR. *The Perspectives of Psychiatry*. Baltimore, MD: Johns Hopkins University Press; 1998.
42. Nye C. Possession, Jinn and Britain's backstreet exorcists. *BBC News*. November 19, 2012. https://www.bbc.com/news/uk-20357997.

CHAPTER 10

1. Wernicke C. *Grundriss der Psychiatriein Klinischen Vorlesungen* [Foundation of Psychiatry in Clinical Lectures]. Leipzig: Fischer & Wittig; 1900.
2. Stokes HS. *The Life and Death of Yukio Mishima*. New York: Cooper Square Press; 2000.
3. Piven J. Phallic narcissism, anal sadism, and oral discord: The case of Yukio Mishima, Part I. *The Psychoanalytic Review*. 2001:88(6):771–91.
4. Editors. Japanese kamikazes died "against their will." *Washington Times*. September 21, 2001. https://www.washingtontimes.com/news/2001/sep/21/20010921-025521-5247r/ (accessed June 4, 2023).
5. Rees L. A kamikaze who lived to tell the tale. *Historynet*. November 28, 2011. https://www.historynet.com/a-kamikaze-who-lived-to-tell-the-tale/ (accessed June 3, 2023).

6. Goertzel TG. Terrorist beliefs and terrorist lives. In: Stout C, ed. *The Psychology of Terrorism*. Westport, CT: Greenwood; 2002:97–112.
7. Woodward B. In Hijacker's Bags, a call to planning, prayer and death. *The Washington Post*. September 27, 2001. https://www.washingtonpost.com/archive/politics/2001/09/28/in-hijackers-bags-a-call-to-planning-prayer-and-death/fd0bd532-6dec-4b98-8979-7ab0e1894e99/ (accessed June 8, 2024).
8. Kristof ND. Islamic "martyrs" in for letdown. *Tampa Bay Times*. August 5, 2004. https://www.tampabay.com/archive/2004/08/05/islamic-martyrs-in-for-a-letdown/ (accessed June 8, 2024).
9. Reid Meloy J. Sexual desire, violent death, and the true believer. *Contemporary Psychoanalysis*. 2018;54(1):64–83.
10. Meloy JR, Gill P. The lone-actor terrorist and the TRAP-18. *Journal of Threat Assessment and Management*. 2016;3:37–52.
11. Post J. Testimony before the Subcommittee on Emerging Threats and Capabilities. United States Senate 107th Congress, November 15, 2001. U.S. Government Printing Office, 2001. https://www.govinfo.gov/content/pkg/CHRG-107shrg79736/html/CHRG-107shrg79736.htm (accessed June 8, 2024).
12. Rahman T. Extreme overvalued beliefs: How violent extremist beliefs become "normalized." *Behavioral Sciences*. 2018;8(1):10.
13. Prakash Kamath DP, Reddy YJ, Kandavel T. Suicidal behavior in obsessive-compulsive disorder. *Journal of Clinical Psychiatry*. 2007;68(11):1741–50.
14. Turecki G, Brent DA, Gunnell D, O'Connor RC, Oquendo MA, Pirkis J, Stanley BH. Suicide and suicide risk. *Nature Reviews Disease Primers*. 2019;5(1):1–22.
15. Erlangsen A, Appadurai V, Wang Y, Turecki G, Mors O, Werge T, Mortensen PB, Starnawska A, Børglum AD, Schork A, Nudel R. Genetics of suicide attempts in individuals with and without mental disorders: A population-based genome-wide association study. *Molecular Psychiatry*. 2020;25(10):2410–21.
16. Hjelmeland, H. Suicide research and prevention: The importance of culture in "biological times." In: Colucci E, Lester D, eds. *Suicide and Culture: Understanding the Context*. Gottingen: Hogrefe; 2013:3–23.
17. Posner K, Brown GK, Stanley B, Brent DA, Yershova KV, Oquendo MA, Currier GW, Melvin GA, Greenhill L, Shen S, Mann JJ. The Columbia–Suicide Severity Rating Scale: Initial validity and internal consistency findings from three multisite studies with adolescents and adults. *American Journal of Psychiatry*. 2011;168(12):1266–77.
18. Durkheim, Emile. *Suicide: A Study in Sociology*. New York: Free Press; 1951.
19. Jamison KR. *Night Falls Fast: Understanding Suicide*. New York: Alfred A. Knoff; 1999.
20. Joiner, Thomas E. *Why People Die by Suicide*. Cambridge, MA: Harvard University Press; 2005.
21. Zorumski C, Rubin E. *Psychiatry and Clinical Neuroscience: A Primer*. New York: Oxford University Press; 2011.
22. Rahman T, Meloy JR, Bauer R: Extreme overvalued belief and the legacy of Carl Wernicke. *The Journal of the American Academy of Psychiatry and the Law*. 2019;47:180–87.
23. American Psychiatric Association. *Diagnostic and Statistical Manual of Mental Disorders*. 5th edition. Arlington, VA: American Psychiatric Press, 2013:286–89.

24. Cohen M. Biden says he thought about suicide after 1972 death of his wife and daughter. *Politico.* August, 17, 2020. https://www.politico.com/news/2020/08/17/biden-contemplated-suicide-after-1972-deaths-wife-daughter-397487 (accessed August 30, 2022).
25. Martikainen P, Valkonen T. Mortality after the death of a spouse: Rates and causes of death in a large Finnish cohort. *American Journal of Public Health.* 1996;86:1087–93.
26. Wilcox HC, Kuramoto SJ, Lichtenstein P, Långström N, Brent DA, Runeson B. Psychiatric morbidity, violent crime, and suicide among children and adolescents exposed to parental death. *Journal of the American Academy of Child & Adolescent Psychiatry.* 2010;49(5):514–23.
27. Li J, Precht DH, Mortensen PB, Olsen J. Mortality in parents after death of a child in Denmark: A nationwide follow-up study. *The Lancet.* 2003;361(9355):363–67.
28. James H. *The Creation and Destruction of Value: The Globalization Cycle.* Cambridge, MA: Harvard University Press; 2009.
29. Klein C. 1929 stock market crash: Did panicked investors really jump from windows? *CNN.* March 7, 2019. https://www.history.com/news/stock-market-crash-suicides-wall-street-1929-great-depression (accessed August 30, 2022).
30. Galbraith JK. *The Great Crash 1929.* New York: Houghton Mifflin Harcourt; 2009.
31. Henne K, Ventresca M. A criminal mind? A damaged brain? Narratives of criminality and culpability in the celebrated case of Aaron Hernandez. *Crime, Media, Culture.* 2020;16(3):395–413.
32. Rashbaum WK, Weiser B, Gold M. Jeffrey Epstein dead in suicide at jail, spurring inquiries. *New York Times.* August 10, 2019. https://www.nytimes.com/2019/08/10/nyregion/jeffrey-epstein-suicide.html (accessed August 30, 2022).
33. Carson AE. Suicide in local jails and state and federal prisons, 2000–2019. Mortality in Local Jails and State Prisons. U.S. Bureau of Justice Statistics . October 2021. https://bjs.ojp.gov/library/publications/suicide-local-jails-and-state-and-federal-prisons-2000–2019-statistical-tables (accessed August 30, 2022).
34. Schonfled Z. After Chester Bennington's death, suicide experts fear a contagion effect. *Newsweek.* July 20, 2017. https://www.newsweek.com/chester-bennington-suicide-linkin-park-chris-cornell-639940 (accessed August 30, 2022).
35. Seeman MV. The Marilyn Monroe group and the Werther effect. *Case Reports Journal.* 2017;1(1):4.
36. Fink DS, Santaella-Tenorio J, Keyes KM. Increase in suicides the months after the death of Robin Williams in the US. *PLoS One.* 2018;13(2):e0191405.
37. Joiner TE Jr. The clustering and contagion of suicide. *Current Directions in Psychological Science.* 1999;8(3):89–92.
38. Hedegaard H, Curtin SC, Warner M. Suicide mortality in the United States, 1999–2019. *NCHS Data Brief.* 2021;3398:1–8. https://www.cdc.gov/nchs/products/databriefs/db398.htm (accessed June 8, 2024.
39. Rahman T. Extreme overvalued beliefs: How violent extremist beliefs become "normalized." *Behavioral Sciences.* 2018;8(1):10.
40. Durkee T, Hadlaczky G, Westerlund M, Carli V. Internet pathways in suicidality: A review of the evidence. *International Journal of Environmental Research and Public Health.* 2011;77(10):3938–52.
41. Ahmadpanah M, Astinsadaf S, Akhondi A, Haghighi M, Bahmani DS, Nazaribadie M, Jahangard L, Holsboer-Trachsler E, Brand S. Early maladaptive schemas of emotional deprivation, social isolation, shame and abandonment are related to

a history of suicide attempts among patients with major depressive disorders. *Comprehensive Psychiatry.* 2017;(77):71–79.

42. Mellor S. After a 14-year-old Instagram user's suicide, Meta apologizes for (some of) the self-harm and suicide content she saw. *Yahoo! News.* September 27, 2022. https://www.yahoo.com/video/14-old-instagram-users-suicide-151102166.html (accessed June 4, 2023).

43. *CBS 60 Minutes Overtime.* Teen watched simulated hanging video on Instagram before suicide. December 11, 2022. https://www.cbsnews.com/news/instagram-hanging-video-suicide-60-minutes-2022-12-11/ (accessed June 3, 2023).

44. Alfonsi S. More than 1,200 families suing social media companies over kids' mental health. *CBS News 60 Minutes.* https://www.cbsnews.com/news/social-media-lawsuit-meta-tiktok-facebook-instagram-60-minutes-2022-12-11/ (accessed June 4, 2023).

45. Sinyor M, Williams M, Zaheer R, Loureiro R, Pirkis J, Heisel MJ, Schaffer A, Redelmeier DA, Cheung AH, Niederkrotenthaler T. The association between Twitter content and suicide. *Australian & New Zealand Journal of Psychiatry.* 2021;55(3):268–76.

46. Picardo J, McKenzie SK, Collings S, Jenkin G. Suicide and self-harm content on Instagram: A systematic scoping review. *PLoS One.* 2020;15(9):e0238603.

CHAPTER 11

1. Rahman T, Meloy JR, Bauer R. Extreme overvalued belief and the legacy of Carl Wernicke. *The Journal of the American Academy of Psychiatry and the Law.* 2019;47:180–87.
2. Dostoyevsky F. *Crime and Punishment.* (Translated by C. Garnett) New York: Barnes and Noble, Inc.; 1994. (Original work published 1866).
3. Rahman T, Lauriello J. Schizophrenia: An overview. *Focus.* 2016;14(3):300–7.
4. Meloy JR. *Violent Attachments.* Northvale, NJ: Aronson; 1992
5. Meloy JR. The theoretical frame. *Contemporary Psychoanalysis.* 2018;54(1):64–83.
6. Jensen AK. Nietzsche and Dostoevsky: On the Verge of Nihilism, written by Paolo Stellino. *The Dostoevsky Journal.* 2018;19(1):85–89.
7. Meloy JR. The operational development and empirical testing of the Terrorist Radicalization Assessment Protocol (TRAP-18). *Journal of Personality Assessment.* 2018;100(5):483–92.
8. Rahman T. Extreme overvalued beliefs: How violent extremist beliefs become "normalized." *Behavioral Sciences.* 2018;8(1):10.
9. Rahman T, Zheng L, Meloy JR. DSM-5 cultural and personality assessment of extreme overvalued beliefs. *Aggression and Violent Behavior.* 2021; 60:101552.
10. Bogaerts A. Rediscovering Nietzsche's Übermensch in Superman as a heroic ideal. In: *Superman and Philosophy: What Would the Man of Steel Do?* 2013:83–100.
11. Knoll M. The Übermensch as social and political task: A study in the continuity of Nietzsche's political thought. *Nietzsche as Political Philosopher.* 2014;3:239.
12. Radeska T. Nietzsche's sister, Elisabeth Förster-Nietzsche, edited her brother's work to fit her own anti-Semitic ideology. *The Vintage News.* August 5, 2017. https://www.thevintagenews.com/2017/08/05/nietzsches-sister-elisabeth-forster-nietzsche-edited-her-brothers-work-to-fit-her-own-anti-semitic-ideology/?edg-c=1 (accessed June 5, 2023).

13. Golomb J, Wistrich RS, eds. *Nietzsche, Godfather of Fascism?: On the Uses and Abuses of a Philosophy*. Princeton, NJ: Princeton University Press; 2009.
14. Bataille G. *On Nietzsche*. Albany: State University of New York Press; 2015.
15. Meloy JR, Hoffmann J, eds. *International Handbook of Threat Assessment*. 2nd edition. New York: Oxford University Press; 2021.
16. Miller A. *The Crucible*. London: Penguin Classics; 2000.
17. Huxley, Aldous. *The Devils of Loudun*. New York: Harper & Brothers; 1953.
18. Stephenson C. The epistemological significance of possession entering the DSM. *History of Psychiatry*. 2015:(3):251–69.
19. Longfellow D. A case of witchcraft; The trial of Urbain Grandier. *Journal of Church and State*. 1999;41(3):609.
20. Blackman L, Walkerdine V. *Mass Hysteria: Critical Psychology and Media Studies*. New York: Bloomsbury; 2017.
21. Goldstein DM, Hall K. Mass hysteria in Le Roy, New York: How brain experts materialized truth and outscienced environmental inquiry. *American Ethnologist*. 2015;42(4):640–57.
22. Stephenson CE. The possessions at Loudun: Tracking the discourse of dissociation. *Journal of Analytical Psychology*. 2017;62(4):544–66.
23. Rapley R. *A Case of Witchcraft: The Trial of Urbain Grandier*. Quebec: McGill-Queen's University Press; 1998.
24. Mishima Y. *Confessions of a Mask*. Translated by M Weatherby. New York: New Directions; 1958.
25. Mishima Y, Bester J. *Sun and Steel*. Palo Alto, CA: Kodansha International; 1970.
26. Mishima Y. *Patriotism*. New York: New Directions; 1995.
27. Sorgenfrei CF. *Mishima on Stage: "The Black Lizard" and Other Plays*. Michigan Monograph Series in Japanese Studies. Ann Arbor: University of Michigan; 2007.
28. Jansen MO, Abdelnour E, Rahman T. Science perspective: Clinical care considerations for bereaved patients: Missouri Medicine 2022;119:9–13.
29. Duke TT. Ovid's Pyramus and Thisbe. *The Classical Journal*. 1971;66(4):320–27.
30. Romeo and Juliet, Act 3, Scene 5.
31. Gupta P. Star crossed lovers commit suicide. *Times of India*. May 24, 2012. https://timesofindia.indiatimes.com/city/mumbai/star-crossed-lovers-commit-suicide/articleshow/13418950.cms (accessed June 4, 2023).
32. Schram J. "Two great people" are going to paradise in heartbreaking note: LIRR suicide leapers were under pressure to break up romance, left behind 2-year-old daughter. *New York Post*. October 20, 2022. https://nypost.com/2013/07/31/two-great-people-are-going-to-paradise-in-heartbreaking-note-lirr-suicide-leapers-were-under-pressure-to-break-up-romance-left-behind-2-year-old-daughter/ (accessed June 4, 2023).

EPILOGUE

1. McHugh P. Genius in a time, place and person. In: Jaspers K. Translated by Hoenig J, Hamilton MW. *General Psychopathology*. Volume 1. Baltimore, MD: Johns Hopkins University Press; 1997:vii.
2. Weiss KJ. At a loss for words: Nosological impotence in the search for justice. *Journal of the American Academy of Psychiatry and the Law*. 2016;44(1):36–40.

3. Finkel NJ. *Insanity on Trial*. Boston: Springer; 1988.
4. Giorgi-Guarnieri D, Janofsky J, Keram E, Lawsky S, Merideth P, Mossman D, Schwartz-Watts D, Scott C, Thompson Jr J, Zonona H. AAPL practice guideline for forensic psychiatric evaluation of defendants raising the insanity defense. *Journal of the American Academy of Psychiatry and the Law*. 2002;30(2):S3–S40.
5. Rahman T. Commentary. *The Journal of the American Academy of Psychiatry and the Law*. 2020;48(3):425.
6. Rahman T, Grellner KA, Harry B, Beck N, Lauriello J. Infanticide in a case of folie à deux. *American Journal of Psychiatry*. 2013;170(10):1110–12.
7. Rahman T, Meloy JR, Bauer R. Extreme overvalued belief and the legacy of Carl Wernicke. *The Journal of the American Academy of Psychiatry and the Law*. 2019;47(2):180–87.
8. Rahman T, Resnick PJ, Harry B. Anders Breivik: Extreme beliefs mistaken for psychosis. *The Journal of the American Academy of Psychiatry and the Law*. 2016;44(1):28–35.
9. Pierre JM. Forensic psychiatry versus the varieties of delusion-like belief. *The Journal of the American Academy of Psychiatry and the Law*. 2020;48(3):327–34.
10. Meloy JR. Unrequited love and the wish to kill: Diagnosis and treatment of borderline erotomania. *Bulletin of the Menninger Clinic*. 1989;53(6):477.
11. Zorumski C, Rubin E. *Psychiatry and Clinical Neuroscience: A Primer*. New York: Oxford University Press; 2011.
12. Shapiro E. Parkland trial: Nikolas Cruz spared death penalty, grieving parents react. *ABC News*. October 13, 2022. https://abcnews.go.com/US/live-updates/parkland-shooter-trial/?id=91379423.
13. Meloy JR, Rahman T. Cognitive-affective drivers of fixation in threat assessment. *Behavioral Sciences & the Law*. 2021;39(2):170–89.
14. Rahman T, Zheng L, Meloy JR. DSM-5 cultural and personality assessment of extreme overvalued beliefs. *Aggression and Violent Behavior*. 2021;60:101552.
15. Stice E, Rohde P, Shaw H. *The Body Project: A Dissonance-Based Eating Disorder Prevention Intervention*. New York: Oxford University Press; 2012.
16. Petersen J, Densley J. *The Violence Project: How to Stop a Mass Shooting*. New York: Abrams; 2021.
17. Rahman T, Hartz SM, Xiong W, Meloy JR, Janofsky J, Harry B, Resnick PJ. Extreme overvalued beliefs. *The Journal of the American Academy of Psychiatry and the Law*. 2020;48(3):319–26.
18. Le Bon G. *The Crowd: A Study of the Popular Mind*. 4th impression. London: T. Fisher Unwin; 1895.
19. Stage C. The online crowd: A contradiction in terms? On the potentials of Gustave Le Bon's crowd psychology in an analysis of affective blogging. *Distinktion: Scandinavian Journal of Social Theory*. 2013;14(2):211–26.
20. IMDb, an Amazon company. https://www.imdb.com/. (accessed June 6, 2024).
21. *Kahler v. Kansas*, 206 L. Ed. 2d 312, 2020.

INDEX

Tables and figures are indicated by an italic *t* and *f* following the page number.

Abrahamsen, David, 62
adjustment disorder, and suicidality, 92
affiliations, identifying in threat assessment, 55
aggression
    novel aggression, 31, 52–53
    and obsessive-compulsive disorder, 17
Akiskal, Hagop, 8–9
Allgemeine Psychopathologie (Jaspers), 40
Alone Together (Turkle), 70
alternative model for personality disorders, 59–60
Amarasingam, Amarnath, 71–72
anchoring bias, 78–79
Angeli, Jacob Chansley, 78
anorexia nervosa
    comorbid conditions, 38
    context and history of, 37–39
    eating disorders, case of Adam Lanza, 65–66
    social media and websites, 38
Argentino, Marc-André, 71–72
Arizona, mass shooting in Tucson, 67
Asch, Solomon, 82
attachment theory, 57
attacks, morally reasoned, 77–86
    and binary bias, 81–82
    and exorcism rituals, 84–86
    Gestalt psychology and, 78–81, 79*f*
    group effects, 82
    and internet cognitive isoforms, 78
    role of emotions in, 82–84
    and social media, 80
Aum Shinrikyo cult, 95
Aurora, Colorado, mass shooting at movie theater in, 67
Austin, Texas, shooting from University clock tower in 1966, 19–20
autism spectrum disorder, 57

Bauer, Pauline, 44
Bauer, Robert, 4
Bennington, Chester, 94–95
bin Laden, Osama, 89–91
binary bias, 81–82
    countering online, 109
body dysmorphic disorder, 39–40
Body Project, 107–8
Boston Marathon Bombing, 2
Branch Davidian compound, in Waco, Texas, 23
Breivik, Anders Behring, 1–2, 22
Broken Mirror, The (Phillips), 39
Buffalo, New York, mass shooting at Tops Friendly Market, 2, 71–73
Bugliosi, Vincent, 48

Capgras syndrome, 33–34
Case Closed (Posner), 49
catathymic homicide, 17–20, 34–35
4Chan online forum, 72
8Chan online forum, 72, 73–74
Charleston, South Carolina, mass shooting at Emanuel African Methodist Episcopal Church, 73
Christchurch, New Zealand, attack on mosques in, 2, 71–72
Ciccone, J. Richard, 15
Cobain, Kurt, 94–95
cognitive-affective drivers, of pathological fixation, 10–11
    case of Andrea Yates, 16
    case of Daniel McNaughton, 14–15
    case of Daniel Soiu, 15–16
    case of Dylann Roof, 21–22
Coleman, Matthew, 78

Colorado
  mass shooting at movie theater in Aurora, 67
  shooting at Columbine High School in Littleton, 67
Columbia-Suicide Severity Rating Scale, 91
Columbine High School, Littleton, Colorado, 67
communities, virtual, 32
Confessions of a Mask (Mishima), 101
conformity experiments, 82
Connecticut, shooting at Sandy Hook Elementary School in Newtown, 63–69
Cornell, Chris, 94–95
creativity, threat assessment and evidence of, 58
Crime and Punishment (Dostoyevsky), 4–5, 97–99
criminal history, and threat assessment, 33, 58
criminal law, and extreme overvalued beliefs, 105–9
  countering online binary bias, 109
  and insanity defense, 106–7
  mitigating or aggravating factor, 107
  prevention of targeted attacks, 107–8
  threat assessment and management, 108–9
Crimo III, Robert, 58
Crowd, The (Le Bon), 109
Crusius, Patrick Wood, 73–74
Cruz, Nikolas, 50, 107
cultural formulation, and threat assessment, 59–60
Cunningham, Mark, 11–12

delusional disorder, 13–14
  erotomanic subtype, 15–16
delusions
  as cognitive-affective drivers of fixation, 14–16
  definition of, 12, 20
  versus extreme overvalued beliefs, 3–4, 7
  lethal fixations from, 11–13
  management of, 33–34
  versus obsessions, 8
  of reference, 15–16
  and targeted attacks, 13
demonic influence, extreme overvalued beliefs in, 84–86
Densley, James, 108
Devils of Loudun, The (Huxley), 99–101. *See also* Salem village witch trials
Diagnostic and Statistical Manual of Mental Disorders, Fifth Edition (DSM-5)
  delusions, definition of, 11
Diagnostic and Statistical Manual of Mental Disorders, Fifth Edition (DSM-5-TR), 3–4, 9
  delusions, definition of, 11
digital subcultures, 70–76
  Adam Lanza and a subculture of mass murder, 63–64
  and attack on church bible study in Charleston, South Carolina, 73
  and attack on market in Buffalo, New York, 71–73
  and mass shooting at Robb Elementary School in Uvalde, Texas, 75
  and mass shooting at Walmart in El Paso, Texas, 73–74
  subcultures *versus* cultures, 70–71
Discord online messaging platform, 71
Dostoyevsky, Fydor, 4–5, 97–99
Drummond, Edward, 14

eating disorders, case of Adam Lanza, 65–66
echo-chambers, and morally reasoned attacks, 80
El Paso, Texas, mass shooting at Walmart in, 73–74
Emanuel African Methodist Episcopal Church, mass shooting at, 73
emotion
  relevance for survival, 83
  role in extreme overvalued beliefs, 21–22
  threat assessment and changes in, 58, 82–84
energy, bursts of, 31
Epstein, Jeffrey, 94
exorcism rituals, and morally reasoned attacks, 84–86

Index

extreme overvalued beliefs
    and body dysmorphic disorder, 39–40
    in case of Cesar Sayoc, 27–28
    case of Lee Harvey Oswald, 48–49
    in case of Malik Hasan, 25–26
    case of Payton Gendron, 72–73
    in case of Timothy McVeigh, 24–25
    versus delusions, 3–4, 7
    elements of, 21–23
    and kamikaze pilots, 88–89
    and lack of counterbalancing
        information, 35
    management of, 35–36
    and online suicide subcultures, 96
    in possession or demonic influence,
        84–86
    process of arriving at, 77
    role of emotions in, 21–22
    targeted attacks and, 13, 107–8
extreme overvalued beliefs, and criminal
        law, 105–9
    countering online binary bias, 109
    insanity defense, 106–7
    mitigating or aggravating factor, 107
    prevention of targeted attacks, 107–8
    threat assessment and management, 108–9
extreme overvalued beliefs, history of
        formal definition, 4–6
    versus "normal-valuedness," 4
    and other disorders with over-idealizing
        values, 6
    from preoccupation to pathology, 6
extreme overvalued beliefs, in literature,
        97–104
    Crime and Punishment, by Fydor
        Dostoyevsky, 97–99
    The Devils of Loudun, by Aldous Huxley,
        99–101
    "Patriotism," a short story by Yukio
        Mishima, 101–2
    romances, 102–4
extreme overvalued beliefs, refining
        definition of, 6–9
    after literature review, 9
    DSM-5 and DSM-5-TR definitions, 9
    pathway to violence, 6–7
    violent true believers, 7

Fish's Outline of Psychiatry, 3
fixations
    delusions as cognitive-affective drivers
        of, 14–16
    and threat assessment, 31, 50
Fleming, Stephen, 80
Florida, mass shooting at Marjorie
        Douglas High School in Parkland, 50
Fort Hood, Texas, mass shooting at, 25–26
Freudenreich, Oliver, 8–9

Galbraith, John Kenneth, 93
Gendron, Payton, 2
    mass shooting at Tops Friendly Market,
        71–73
Gestalt psychology, and morally reasoned
        attacks, 78–81, 79f
Goebbels, Joseph, 83–84
Goldwater Rule, ix–x
Great Crash 1929, The (Galbraith), 93
group effects, and morally reasoned
        attacks, 82
*Grundriss der Psychiatrie in klinischen
        Vorlesungen* (Wernicke), 92
Gull, William, 37

Hamas, 21
Harris, Eric, 67
Hasan, Malik, 25–26, 107
Heaven's Gate cult, 95
Hernandez, Aaron, 94
Highland Park, Illinois, Fourth of July
        parade shooting in, 58
Hinckley Jr., John, 106–7
Hitmen for Hire, 67
Holmes, James, 67
Holmes, Oliver Wendell, 80–81, 105–6
Homegrown (Toobin), 24
Huxley, Aldous, 99–101

identifications, used in threat assessment,
        31, 50–51, 74–75, 76
ideological framing, 98
ideology, threat assessment and, 32, 54–55
Illinois, Fourth of July parade shooting in
        Highland Park, 58
incarceration, suicide after, 94

Inconvenient Truth, The (Crusius), 74
innovation, threat assessment and evidence of, 58
insanity defense, 106–7
International Classification of Diseases (ICD-11)
   delusion, definition of, 11
internet cognitive isoform, 66
   and morally reasoned attacks, 78, 83
Islamic State, 21
isomorphism, definition of, 79

Jamison, Kay Redfield, 91–92
January 6, 2021, attack on U. S. Capitol
   attitudes toward, 8–9
   and Sovereign Citizen movement, 44
   and violent true believers, 8
Jaspers, Karl, 7
   causation of targeted attacks, 105
   delusion, definition of, 12
   on querulants, 40
John F. Kennedy, threat assessment and thwarting assassination of, 60–61
Joiner, Thomas, 91–92
Jonestown, Guyana, 95

kamikaze pilots, 88–89
Kelley, Thomas J., 48
King, Robert, 64
Klebold, Dylan, 67
Kraepelin, Emil, 41–42

Langman, Peter, 67
Lanza, Adam, 63–69
   eating disorders, 65–66
   hypothetical trial of, 68–69
   internet cognitive isoform, acquisition of, 66
   mental health history, 64–65
   obsessions, 65–68
   and a subculture of mass murder, 63–64
Las Vegas, Nevada, mass shooting in, 44–45
Le Bon, Gustave, 109
leak, informational, 31, 74–75, 76
Lester, Grant, 41

lethal fixations
   definition of, 29
   and delusional disorder, 13–14
   from delusions, 11–13
   from obsessions, 18–20
literature, extreme overvalued beliefs in, 97–104
   Crime and Punishment, by Fydor Dostoyevsky, 97–99
   The Devils of Loudun, by Aldous Huxley, 99–101
   "Patriotism," a short story by Yukio Mishima, 101–2
   romances, 102–4
Littleton, Colorado, shooting at Columbine High School, 67
live streaming, and online subcultures, 72
Loughner, Jared, 67
love, unrequited love, 5

Mailer, Norman, 51
manifesto, targeted violent
   of Dylann Roof, 73
   of Patrick Crusius, 74
   of Payton Gendron, 71–72
Manshreck, Theo C., 13
"Mass Media Reporting and Enabling of Mass Shooters" (Murray), 67–68
mass shootings
   common characteristics in, 2–4
   locations, public memory of, 1
Massachusetts, Salem village witch trials, 84. *See also* Devils of Loudun, The (Huxley)
McHugh, Paul R., 8, 105
McNaughton, Daniel, 14–15
McNaughton Rules, 15
McVeigh, Timothy, 23–25, 55
Meloy, J. Reid, 7, 15–16, 90
mental illness, identifying in threat assessment, 55–57
Minassin, Alex, 68
Mishima, Yukio, 88, 101–2
Moorish-American Sovereign Citizens, 44
moral outrage, as driver of violence, 5–6, 21–22, 54
   case of Cesar Sayoc, 27–28
   case of Lee Harvey Oswald, 49

case of Timothy McVeigh, 23
and threat assessment, 32
morally reasoned attacks, 77–86
and binary bias, 81–82
and exorcism rituals, 84–86
Gestalt psychology and, 78–81, 79f
group effects, 82
and internet cognitive isoforms, 78
role of emotions in, 82–84
and social media, 80
Moreselli, Enrico, 39
Movement for the Restoration of the Ten Commandments of God doomsday cult, 95
Mullen, Paul E., 41, 42–43
Murray, Jennifer, 67–68

Nevada, mass shooting in Las Vegas, 44–45
New York, mass shooting at Tops Friendly Market in Buffalo, 2, 71–73
New Zealand, attack on mosques in Christchurch, 2, 71–72
Newtown, Connecticut, shooting at Sandy Hook Elementary School, 63–69
Nichols, Terry, 23
Nietzsche, Friedrich, 98–99
Night Falls (Jamison), 91–92
Norway, shooting by Anders Behring Breivik, 1–2, 22

obsessions, 16–18
and catathymic homicide, 17–20
definition of, 16–17, 20
versus delusions, 8
from lethal fixations, case histories, 18–20
management of, 34–35
obsessive-compulsive disorder, 17
occupational functioning, deterioration in, 10–11, 29
thwarting of occupational goals, 32, 55
OCEAN, and human personality traits, 59–60
Oklahoma City bombing, case history, 23–25
online subcultures, 70–76

Adam Lanza and a subculture of mass murder, 63–64
and attack on church bible study in Charleston, South Carolina, 73
and attack on market in Buffalo, New York, 71–73
and mass shooting at Robb Elementary School in Uvalde, Texas, 75
and mass shooting at Walmart in El Paso, Texas, 73–74
subcultures *versus* cultures, 70–71
Oslo, Norway, shooting by Anders Behring Breivik, 1–2, 22
Oswald, Lee Harvey, 46–62
changes in thinking and emotion, 58
childhood of, 55–57
diagnostic considerations, 59–60
extreme overvalued beliefs of, 48–49
history of criminal violence, 58
life in context of threat assessment, 46–47
personality organization, 59–60
self-injurious behaviors, 47–48
sharp-shooting skills, 51
tactical thinking, creativity and innovation in, 58
threat assessment and thwarting assassination of John F. Kennedy, 60–61
trail, and sentencing considerations, 61–62
Oswald, Lee Harvey, warning signs missed, 50–58
eight positive distal characteristics, 54–58
five proximal warnings, 50–53
Oswald's Tale (Mailer), 51
Oxford Textbook of Psychiatry, 3

Paddock, Stephen, 44–45
pair bonding, threat assessment and, 32, 90
paranoia querulants, 41–42
Parker, George F., 44
Parkland, Florida, shooting at Marjorie Douglas High School, 50

pathological fixations
  definition of, 29
  delusions as cognitive-affective drivers of, 14–16
  management of, 33–36
pathological fixations, and overvalued ideas, 10–11
  and delusional disorder, 13–14
  and delusions, 11–13
pathway, identifying in threat assessment, 51–52
Patriot Movement, 23
"Patriotism" (Mishima), 101–2
Peel, Robert, 14
personal grievance, as driver of violence, 5–6, 54
  case of Lee Harvey Oswald, 49
  and threat assessment, 32
personality organization, case of Lee Harvey Oswald, 59–60
Peterson, Jillian, 108
Phillips, Katherine, 39
Pierce, William, 23
Pierre, Joseph, 106
pipe bombs, mailings by Cesar Sayoc, 26–28
Posner, Gerald, 49
Post, Jerrold, 90
Puckett, Kathleen, 55
Purdy, Patrick, 66

QAnon, 44
  and morally reasoned attacks, 78
querulants, or vexatious litigators, 40–43
  categories of severity, 42–43
  paranoia querulants, 41–42
  querulous discourse, 42

Ramos, Salvador, 2–3, 10–11
Rathjen, Tobias, 36
Reclaiming History (Bugliosi), 48
replacement theory, definition of, 71
research, into threat assessment, 33
Resnick, Phillip, 16
Robb Elementary School, Uvalde, Texas, 2–3, 75
Rodger, Elliot, 83–84

romance, and extreme overvalued beliefs, 102–4
Romeo and Juliet (Shakespeare), 103
Roof, Dylann, 21–22, 49, 73
Russell, Molly, 96

Salem village witch trials, 84. *See also* Devils of Loudun, The (Huxley)
Sandy Hook Elementary School, Newtown, Connecticut, 63–69
Sayoc, Cesar, 26–28
schemas, intellectual growth and, 80
Schneider, Kurt, 7–8, 12–13
Sea of Fertility, The (Mishima), 88
self-injurious behaviors, Lee Harvey Oswald and, 47–48
seppuku, ritualized suicide, 87–88
September 11, 2001, terrorist attacks of, 7–8
  attitudes toward, 8–9
  martyrdom and suicide, 89–91
  subsequent threat analysis methods, 29
  and violent true believers, 7
Shakespeare, William, 103
Silver, James, 14
Sims, Andrew, 3, 7–8, 37
social functioning, deterioration in, 10–11, 29
social media
  algorithms, 35, 80
  and anorexia nervosa websites, 38
  and online suicide subcultures, 96
  and virtual communities, 32, 72
Soiu, Daniel, 15–16
South Carolina, mass shooting at Emanuel African Methodist Episcopal Church in Charleston, 73
Sovereign Citizens, 43–44
Stephenson, Craig, 100–1
suicide, 87–96
  after incarceration, 94
  after loss of a fortune, 93–94
  after the death of a loved one, 92–93
  and a collective identity, 87–89, 90–91
  martyrdom and attacks of September 11, 2001, 89–91
  mass clusters and point clusters, 95

and online subcultures, 96
as public health concern, 91
seppuku, ritualized suicide, 87–88
suicidality and subcultures, 91–92
suicide contagion, 94–96
Sun and Steel (Mishima), 101
"Surfing for Thinness," 38
Symptoms in the Mind (Sims), 3, 37

tactical thinking, creativity and innovation in, 33, 58
targeted attacks
　case of Timothy McVeigh, 24–25
　and delusions *versus* overvalued ideas, 13
　and identification with militaristic or violent groups, 22
　and ideological framing, 98
　and pathological fixation, 10–11
　prevention of, 107–8
Tarrant, Brenton Harrison, 2, 71–72
terrorism, characteristics of lone actors, 25, 27
Terrorist Radicalization Assessment Protocol (TRAP-18)
　applying to case of Lee Harvey Oswald, 50–58
　development of, 29
　distal characteristics, 30t, 32–33
　parts of, 30t
　peer-reviewed research, 33
　proximal warning behaviors, 30t, 31–32
　See also threat assessment; threat management, pathological fixations and
Texas
　mass shooting at Fort Hood, 25–26
　mass shooting at Robb Elementary School in Uvalde, 2–3, 75
　mass shooting at Walmart in El Paso, 73–74
thinking, threat assessment and changes in, 58, 82–84
threat assessment
　criminal history, 33, 58
　energy, bursts of, 31
　and extreme overvalued beliefs in literature, 99

fixations in, 31, 50
ideology and, 32, 54–55
leak, informational, 31, 74–75
and management, 108–9
mental illness, 55–57
missed warning signs, 74–75
moral outrage and personal grievance, 32, 54
novel aggression, 31, 52–53
and pair bonding, 32, 90
and pathway to violence, 51–52
self or group identifications, 31, 50–51, 74–75, 76
tactical thinking, creativity and innovation in, 33, 58
and thwarting assassination of John F. Kennedy, 60–61
and thwarting of occupational goals, 32, 55
See also Terrorism Radicalization Assessment Protocol (TRAP-18)
threat management, pathological fixations and, 33–36
　delusions, 33–34
　extreme overvalued beliefs, 35–36
　obsessions, 34–35
Toobin, Jeffrey, 24
triggering event, identifying in threat assessment, 53–54
Tritico, Chris, 24
Tsarnaev, Dzhokhar, 2
Tucson, Arizona, mass shooting in, 67
Turkle, Sherry, 70
Turner Diaries, The (Pierce), 23

Ueber den Querulantenwahnsinn (Kraepelin), 41–42
unrequited love, and extreme overvalued beliefs, 5
Uvalde, Texas, mass shooting at Robb Elementary School, 2–3, 75

Veale, David, 13
vexatious litigators, or querulants, 40–43
　categories of severity, 42–43
　paranoia querulants, 41–42
　querulous discourse, 42
violence, pathway to, 6–7, 51–52

Violence Project, 108
violent grievances, 44–45
　and January 6, 2021 attack on U. S. Capitol, 44
　and Las Vegas mass shooting, 44–45
violent true believers, 7
　case of Timothy McVeigh, 24–25
virtual communities, 32
　dependence on, 72

Waco, Texas, Branch Davidian compound in, 23
Walker, Edwin, 52
warning signs, missed, 74–75
Weiss, Ken, 105
Wernicke, Carl
　on Dostoyevsky's *Crime and Punishment*, 97, 98
and history of formal EOB definition, 4–6
insanity defense, 106
and refining definition of EOB, 6–8
role of emotions in EOB, 22
suicide and overvalued ideas, 92
whistle-blowers *versus* vexatious litigators, 40–41
White, Stephen, 40–41
Whitman, Charles, 19–20
Why People Die by Suicide (Joiner), 91–92
Winokur, George, 13
witch trials, Salem village, 84. *See also* Devils of Loudun, The (Huxley)

Yates, Andrea, 16

Zawahiri, Ayman al-, 89–90